CLARA
BARTON

AMERICAN WOMEN of ACHIEVEMENT

CLARA BARTON

LENI HAMILTON

CHELSEA HOUSE PUBLISHERS

PHILADELPHIA

EDITOR-IN-CHIEF: Nancy Toff
EXECUTIVE EDITOR: Remmel T. Nunn
MANAGING EDITOR: Karyn Gullen Browne
COPY CHIEFS: Juliann Barbato,
            Perry Scott King
ART DIRECTOR: Giannella Garrett

Staff for CLARA BARTON:

TEXT EDITOR: Rick Rennert
ASSISTANT EDITOR: Maria Behan
EDITORIAL ASSISTANT: Karen Schimmel
COPYEDITORS: Gillian Bucky, Sean Dolan
DESIGN: Design Oasis
PICTURE RESEARCH: Cheryl Moch, Diane Wallis
PRODUCTION COORDINATOR: Alma Rodriguez
COVER ILLUSTRATION: © Michael Garland

CREATIVE DIRECTOR: Harold Steinberg

9

Library of Congress Cataloging in Publication Data

Hamilton, Leni. CLARA BARTON

(American women of achievement)
Bibliography: p.
Includes index.
1. Barton, Clara, 1821–1912—Juvenile literature. 2. Red Cross—
Biography—Juvenile literature. 3. American National Red Cross—
Juvenile literature. 4. Nurses—United States—Biography—
Juvenile literature. [1. Barton, Clara, 1821–1912. 2. Nurses
3. American National Red Cross]
I. Title. II. Series.
HV569.B3H35   1987   361.7′634′0924 [B] [92]   87-5158

ISBN 1-55546-641-9
      0-7910-0409-0 (pbk.)

CONTENTS

WOMEN OF ACHIEVEMENT

Abigail Adams
WOMEN'S RIGHTS ADVOCATE

Jane Addams
SOCIAL WORKER

Madeleine Albright
STATESWOMAN

Louisa May Alcott
AUTHOR

Marian Anderson
SINGER

Susan B. Anthony
WOMAN SUFFRAGIST

Ethel Barrymore
ACTRESS

Clara Barton
AMERICAN RED CROSS FOUNDER

Elizabeth Blackwell
PHYSICIAN

Pearl Buck
AUTHOR

Margaret Bourke-White
PHOTOGRAPHER

Rachel Carson
BIOLOGIST AND AUTHOR

Mary Cassatt
ARTIST

Hillary Rodham Clinton
FIRST LADY/ATTORNEY

Diana, Princess of Wales
HUMANITARIAN

Emily Dickinson
POET

Isadora Duncan
DANCER

Amelia Earhart
AVIATOR

Betty Friedan
FEMINIST

Althea Gibson
TENNIS CHAMPION

Helen Hayes
ACTRESS

Katharine Hepburn
ACTRESS

Anne Hutchinson
RELIGIOUS LEADER

Mahalia Jackson
GOSPEL SINGER

Helen Keller
HUMANITARIAN

Jeane Kirkpatrick
DIPLOMAT

Barbara McClintock
BIOLOGIST

Margaret Mead
ANTHROPOLOGIST

Edna St. Vincent Millay
POET

Agnes de Mille
CHOREOGRAPHER

Julia Morgan
ARCHITECT

Grandma Moses
PAINTER

Georgia O'Keeffe
PAINTER

Sandra Day O'Connor
SUPREME COURT JUSTICE

Rosie O'Donnell
ENTERTAINER/COMEDIENNE

Eleanor Roosevelt
DIPLOMAT AND HUMANITARIAN

Wilma Rudolph
CHAMPION ATHLETE

Gloria Steinem
FEMINIST

Harriet Beecher Stowe
AUTHOR AND ABOLITIONIST

Elizabeth Taylor
ACTRESS/ACTIVIST

Barbara Walters
JOURNALIST

Edith Wharton
AUTHOR

Phyllis Wheatley
POET

Babe Didrikson Zaharias
CHAMPION ATHLETE

"Remember the Ladies"

MATINA S. HORNER

Remember the Ladies." That is what Abigail Adams wrote to her husband John, then a delegate to the Continental Congress, as the Founding Fathers met in Philadelphia to form a new nation in March of 1776. "Be more generous and favorable to them than your ancestors. Do not put such unlimited power in the hands of the Husbands. If particular care and attention is not paid to the Ladies," Abigail Adams warned, "we are determined to foment a Rebellion, and will not hold ourselves bound by any Laws in which we have no voice, or Representation."

The words of Abigail Adams, one of the earliest American advocates of women's rights, were prophetic. Because when we have not "remembered the ladies," they have, by their words and deeds, reminded us so forcefully of the omission that we cannot fail to remember them. For the history of American women is as interesting and varied as the history of our nation as a whole. American women have played an integral part in founding, settling, and building our country. Some we remember as remarkable women who—against great odds—achieved distinction in the public arena: Anne Hutchinson, who in the 17th century became a charismatic religious leader; Phillis Wheatley, an 18th-century black slave who became a poet; Susan B. Anthony, whose name is synonymous with the 19th-century women's rights movement, and who led the struggle to enfranchise women; and, in our own century, Amelia Earhart, the first woman to cross the Atlantic Ocean by air.

These extraordinary women certainly merit our admiration, but other women, "common women," many of them all but forgotten, should also be recognized for their contributions to American thought and culture. Women have been community builders; they have founded schools and formed voluntary associations to help those in need; they have assumed the major responsibility for rearing children, passing on from one generation to the next the values that keep a culture alive. These and innumerable other contributions, once ignored, are now being recognized by scholars, students, and the public. It is exciting and gratifying to realize that a part of our history that was hardly acknowledged a few generations ago is now being studied and brought to light.

In recent decades, the field of women's history has grown from obscurity to a politically controversial splinter movement to academic respectability, in many cases mainstreamed into such traditional disciplines as history, economics, and psychology. Scholars of women, both female and male, have organized research centers at such prestigious institutions as Wellesley College, Stanford University, and the University of California. Other notable centers for women's studies are the Center for the American Woman and Politics at the Eagleton Institute of Politics at Rutgers University, the Henry A. Murray Research Center for the Study of Lives, at Radcliffe College, and the Women's Research and Education Institute, the research arm of the Congressional Caucus on Women's Issues. Other scholars and public figures have established archives and libraries, such as the Schlesinger Library on the History of Women in America, at Radcliffe College, and the Sophia Smith Collection, at Smith College, to collect and preserve the written and tangible legacies of women.

From the initial donation of the Women's Rights Collection in 1943, the Schlesinger Library grew to encompass vast collections documenting the manifold accomplishments of American women. Simultaneously, the women's movement in general and the academic discipline of women's studies in particular also began with a narrow definition and gradually expanded their mandate. Early causes such as woman suffrage and social reform, abolition and organized labor were joined by newer concerns such as the history of women in business and the professions and in politics and government; the study of the family; and social issues such as health policy and education.

Women, as historian Arthur M. Schlesinger, jr., once pointed out, "have constituted the most spectacular casualty of traditional history. They have made up at least half the human race, but you could never tell that by looking at the books historians write." The new breed of historians is remedying that omission. They have written books about immigrant women and about working-class women who struggled for survival in cities and about black women who met the challenges of life in rural areas. They are telling the stories of women who, despite the barriers of tradition and economics, became lawyers and doctors and public figures.

The women's studies movement has also led scholars to question traditional interpretations of their respective disciplines. For example, the study of war has traditionally been an exercise in military and political analysis, an examination of strategies planned and executed by men. But scholars of women's history have pointed out that wars have also been periods of tremendous change and even opportunity for women, because the very absence of men on the home front enabled them to expand their educational, economic, and professional activities and to assume leadership in their homes.

The early scholars of women's history showed a unique brand of courage in choosing to investigate new subjects and take new approaches to old ones. Often, like their subjects, they endured criticism and even ostracism by their academic colleagues. But their efforts have unquestionably been worthwhile, because with the publication of each new study and book another piece of the historical patchwork is sewn into place, revealing an increasingly comprehensive picture of the role of women in our rich and varied history.

Such books on groups of women are essential, but books that focus on the lives of individuals are equally indispensable. Biographies can be inspirational, offering their readers the example of people with vision who have looked outside themselves for their goals and have often struggled against great obstacles to achieve them. Marian Anderson, for instance, had to overcome racial bigotry in order to perfect her art and perform as a concert singer. Isadora Duncan defied the rules of classical dance to find true artistic freedom. Jane Addams had to break down society's notions of the proper role for women in order to create new social institutions, notably the settlement house. All of these women had to come to terms both with themselves and with the world in which they lived. Only then could they move ahead as pioneers in their chosen callings.

Biography can inspire not only by adulation but also by realism. It helps us to see not only the qualities in others that we hope to emulate, but also, perhaps, the weaknesses that made them "human." By helping us identify with the subject on a more personal level they help us to feel that we, too, can achieve such goals. We read about Eleanor Roosevelt, for instance, who occupied a unique and seemingly enviable position as the wife of the president. Yet we can sympathize with her inner dilemma: an inherently shy woman, she had to force herself to live a most public life in order to use her position to benefit others. We may not be able to imagine ourselves having the immense poetic talent of Emily Dickinson, but from her story we can understand the challenges faced by a creative woman who was expected to fulfill many family responsibilities. And though few of us will ever reach the level of athletic accomplishment displayed by Wilma Rudolph or Babe Zaharias, we can still appreciate their spirit, their overwhelming will to excel.

A biography is a multifaceted lens. It is first of all a magnification, the intimate examination of one particular life. But at the same time, it is a wide-angle lens, informing us about the world in which the subject lived. We come away from reading about one life knowing more about the social, political, and economic fabric of the time. It is for this reason, perhaps, that the great New England essayist Ralph Waldo Emerson wrote, in 1841, "There is properly no history: only biography." And it is also why biography, and particularly women's biography, will continue to fascinate writers and readers alike.

CLARA BARTON

Clara Barton's strong sense of purpose enabled her to overcome her basically shy nature and become a leading figure in many humanitarian causes.

ONE

A Surprising Figure

All afternoon the wounded had been carried by mule-drawn wagons to the wooded slope near the train station. Piles of hay had been scattered over the ground, and the torn and bleeding bodies had been laid upon the piles. The soldiers were often packed so closely together that there was scarcely enough space to walk between them. On this late summer day in 1862, in the second year of the War Between the States—the Civil War—death, the grim reaper, had brought in a full harvest on the fields of Chantilly, Virginia.

When night fell, the terrain was lit up by the flames of small candles. Many of those among the wounded soldiers who remained conscious were surprised to see a small, thin, straight-backed woman moving among them with bandages and dressings. Wearing a dark hoopless skirt and calico blouse, she was barely five feet tall, with thick, black hair. They guessed her age at about 40. Who she was and how she had gotten there they could not imagine, for it was simply unthinkable that a female nurse could be at the battlefront. Everyone knew that such a thing was forbidden. Yet there she was, covering cold feet with warm slippers, wrapping blankets over shivering bodies, binding up wounds with clean dressings, and offering hot meals, which appeared as if by magic.

Clara Barton was too busy to notice that there were curious eyes upon her. By chance she looked up and saw the flickering light of a lantern approaching. It was held by one of the surgeons. In the journal that she would keep for more than 60 years she recorded his words to her.

"Lady," he said as he drew near, "will you go with me? Out on the hills is a

Barton tends to a wounded soldier during the Civil War.

poor distressed lad, mortally wounded and dying. His piteous cries for his sister have touched all our hearts, and none of us can relieve him, but rather seem to distress him by our presence."

Rising from her tasks, Barton stepped between the prostrate bodies and followed the surgeon up the side of the hill. In the darkness she could still see both Confederate and Union soldiers collecting their dead under a flag of truce.

"He can't last half an hour longer," the surgeon said. "He is already quite cold, shot through the abdomen, a terrible wound." By this time Barton could plainly hear the soldier's cries.

"Mary, Mary, sister Mary, come—oh,

come, I am wounded. Mary! I am shot. I am dying—oh, come to me—I have called you so long and my strength is almost gone. Don't let me die here alone. Oh Mary, Mary, come!"

The boy's name was Hugh Johnson. He was thin and slight, with pale skin and long hair that was tangled and matted. His large bewildered eyes turned in every direction. Barton bent down and touched his neck, then kissed his forehead and laid her cheek next to his.

"Oh, Mary! Mary! You have come? I knew you would come if I called and I have called you so long. I could not die without you, Mary. Don't cry, darling. I am not afraid to die now that you have come to me. Oh, bless you. Bless you, Mary."

Barton said later, "I can never forget that cry of joy." She drew her warm shawl around his shoulders and put her arms around him. For a moment she was tempted to speak the word "brother" to him, but the word would not come to her lips. She was still holding him in her arms when the first red rays of dawn pierced the night sky. She noted:

"Of course the morning light would reveal his mistake, but he had grown calm and was refreshed and able to endure it, and when finally he woke, he seemed puzzled for a moment, but then he smiled and said: 'I knew before I opened my eyes that this couldn't be Mary. I know now that she couldn't get

By mid-1862, the sight of Barton giving aid on the battlefield had become a familiar one to Union soldiers.

here, but it is almost as good. You've made me so happy.' "

Barton would later learn when she visited the infirmary in Washington, D.C., that the soldier had lived for two more days, long enough to say farewell to his family. But at that moment in the morning she could only feel simple gratitude for the chance to close her eyes. Her hour's sleep holding Hugh Johnson was the first rest she had had in three days.

Yet 3,000 men still needed her. They had nothing to eat but the food Barton had brought them. And the Union army had said it needed no supplies! The army had said it had no need for nurses!

15

Captain Stephen Barton was a man of many talents and several occupations. He was a soldier, a farmer, an administrator, and an elected government official.

TWO

The Child Nurse

Captain Stephen Barton's story of survival had become familiar to his daughter Clara. Wounded in battle deep in the tangled marshes of Michigan, he had found himself alone, without food or water. Facing what was almost certain death, he had suddenly seen a hoofprint in the mud with water oozing in it. His miraculous discovery of the water, along with the appearance of a starving dog, which became the captain's supper, were the reasons he survived to tell the tale.

The captain was a kindly looking, gray-haired man in his late fifties, and the 11-year-old girl listening raptly to her father's story could hardly imagine him as a 19-year-old, noncommissioned officer fighting out west in his country's Indian wars. From his glorified accounts, Clara Barton learned the intricacies of battlefield strategy and military etiquette. She was to recall in her memoirs that such instruction had not lacked value for her.

> When later, I . . . was suddenly thrust into the mysteries of war, and had to find and take my place and part in it, I . . . never addressed a colonel as captain, got my cavalry on foot, or mounted my infantry.

The youngest of the five Barton children, Clarissa Harlowe Barton was her doting father's favorite. It is possible that he considered her birth a special gift, since she made her appearance in the world on Christmas Day in 1821. A prosperous farmer, Barton had been elected both as the chief administrative authority of the town of Oxford, Massachusetts, and as a representative to the state legislature. He was gentle and philanthropic by nature. When his nephew, Jeremiah Learned, died, leaving behind a wife and four children, Barton and another relative purchased

According to Barton, her mother ran the household with such efficiency and energy that she "always did two days' work in one."

the farm in 1830 in order to save the widow from becoming destitute. Moving his family to the new homestead, Barton not only took in the widow and her children but also the orphaned young son of an old friend. Her father's humanitarian outlook appears to have been the major force in the molding of Clara's character.

Clara's mother was a plump, plain, no-nonsense woman who was nearly 40 when Clara was born. Sally Stone Barton had straight black hair parted neatly down the middle and drawn back into a tight bun. She was practical,

firm, and efficient, forbidding Clara such frivolities as dolls and toys but instead teaching her invaluable lessons in household management and organization.

The Barton family's second youngest daughter, also named Sally, was already 12 years old when Clara was born. Growing up in the Barton household, Clara sometimes felt as if she had six parents. Three of her siblings—Dorothy, Stephen, and Sally—grew up to become schoolteachers. From Dorothy, the oldest, Clara learned how to read. Her brother Stephen taught her mathematics. Sally taught her geography. By the time Clara entered Colonel Richard Stone's one-room schoolhouse when she was four, she could already spell words like *artichoke*.

It was Clara's brother David, however, who was her special favorite. A natural athlete whose passion was horses, David taught Clara to ride when she was scarcely more than three years old. She wrote of him:

I recall vividly the half impatient frown on his fine face when he would see me do an awkward thing, however trivial. He detested false motions, wanted the thing done rightly the first time.... If I would drive a nail, strike it fairly on the head every time, and not split the board. If I would draw a screw, turn it right the first time. I must tie a square knot that would hold and not tie my horse with a slip noose and leave him to choke himself. These were little things, still a part of the instructions not to be undervalued. In the rather

Barton was born in this house in North Oxford, Massachusetts.

When Barton was nine years old, she moved with her family to this home, also in North Oxford, Massachusetts.

Barn raisings such as the one shown here were usually social as well as practical events.

practical life which has sometimes fallen to me, I have wondered if they were not among the most useful, and if that handsome frown were not one of my best lessons.

Blessed with intelligence and an aptitude for schoolwork, Clara was also hypersensitive and shy. Even at the First Universalist Church, which the Bartons helped to found and which the family attended without fail every week, she stayed close to her mother's skirts. Wishing to help her overcome her shyness, Clara's parents sent her away to boarding school when she was nine years old. But Clara did not do well there. Hearing that the child was

eating poorly, the Bartons decided to bring her home.

In the summer of 1832, at the age of 10, Clara witnessed a near tragedy that befell her beloved brother David. The Bartons were hosting a barn raising on their homestead, a social event attended by friends and neighbors who had come to assist the family. It was while they were attaching the rafters of the new barn that David fell from the ridgepole at the very top of the new roof. Clara remembered how her brother fell, landing feetfirst on a timber near the bottom of the cellar:

> Without falling he leaped to the ground, and after a few breathless moments declared himself unhurt but was not permitted to return aloft. It was spoken of as a "remarkable adventure" and for a few days all went well with the exception of David's slight and quite unaccustomed headache, which continued to increase as the July weather progressed. At length he showed symptoms of a fever....

The family physician, along with another doctor, were subsequently consulted about David's illness. Relying on their primitive medical knowledge, these doctors believed that David's persistent fever was the result of his having "too much blood" and of being "too vigorous" in constitution. It was their considered opinion that the only way David would ever get over the fever was if they were to "bleed" him. This procedure was accomplished in those days by applying bloodsucking leeches to various parts of the unfortunate patient's body.

Barton recalled:

> From the first days and nights of illness I remained near his side. I could not be taken away from him, except by compulsion, and he was unhappy until my return. I learned to take all directions for his medicines from his physicians (who had eminent counsel) and to administer them like a genuine nurse. My little hands became schooled to the handling of the great loathsome, crawly leeches who were at first so many snakes to me, and no fingers could so painlessly dress the angry blisters, and thus it came about that I was the accepted and acknowledged nurse of a man almost too ill to recover.

The small building at the left served as the office for David and Stephen Barton's successful milling business.

After several weeks of bloodletting treatment David showed no improvement. Two more doctors informed the elder Bartons that their son's case was hopeless. But Clara refused to give up on him. She read to David and tried to cheer him up. She washed his body and fed him from a spoon. For the next two years she rarely left his bedside.

One day a new doctor, Asa McCullum, came to examine David. McCullum was a follower of a physician named Samuel Thompson, who was generally considered to be a quack by the respected physicians of the day. Thompson and his followers were called "the Steam Doctors" because they believed that steam baths, or "hydrotherapy," were beneficial to their patients. They also held the revolutionary view that nobody could have "too much blood" or be "too vigorous" and that bleeding a patient was both harmful and unnecessary.

McCullum took David away with him to his sanatorium 20 miles outside of Oxford to begin hydrotherapy. He discontinued not only the bleeding but also David's other medications. In three weeks David was able to return home, and in six weeks he was fully recovered. Whether it was the steam baths that had cured him or simply the respite from harmful medical treatments no one could say with certainty. One thing only was very clear: David owed his life to his little sister, who had given him constant support and willed that he live.

While Barton was a student at Clinton Liberal Institute, she worked hard at her studies, taking advantage of the opportunity to receive a well-rounded education.

THREE

School Days

Clara was home from school with the mumps. She had dozed off on the lounge in the sitting room while her parents were entertaining a house-guest. The guest was one of the many speakers on the New England lecture circuit who somehow always seemed to show up at the Barton household. Awakening from her slumber, the 15-year-old girl was surprised to discover that the guest was talking to her parents about her.

"The sensitive nature will always remain," he said. "She will never assert herself for herself; she will suffer wrong first—but for others she will be perfectly fearless."

"What shall I do?" Clara heard her mother ask.

"Throw responsibility on her, and when she is old enough, give her a school to teach."

The guest's name was Lorenzo Niles Fowler. Both he and his brother, Orson, were famous for their ideas on such matters as marriage, love, philosophy, ethics, civilization, alcohol, tobacco, the bodily organs, and health. They claimed to have obtained their knowledge through the "science" of phrenology, a study of the physical anatomy of the human skull. It is, in fact, a study more than slightly tinged with quackery. But there is no doubt that Lorenzo Fowler exerted a major influence on Clara Barton. His book *Mental Science as Explained by Phrenology* launched her into a lifelong interest in the workings of the human mind. This—and her study of philosophy—gave her an insight into people that was to prove useful throughout her life.

Coming from a family of school-teachers, Barton would no doubt have followed that profession even without

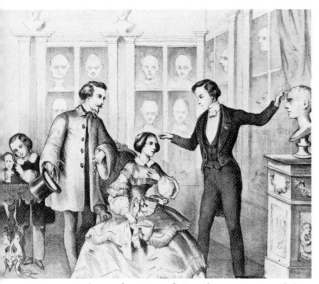

A phrenologist explains the anatomy of the human skull in this lithograph, circa 1830.

Fowler's advice. She enjoyed learning, and as teaching in the 19th century did not require college-level education, she applied for her teaching certification when she was only 17 years old. On May 5, 1839, she stood before an examining committee consisting of a clergyman, a lawyer, and a judge. Passing her oral exam with flying colors, she was swiftly appointed to a teaching position in North Oxford, Massachusetts, at District School No. 9.

Barton approached her first day in front of a class with a feeling of terror. A teenager who had barely overcome the shyness of her youth, she felt almost paralyzed with self-doubt. She had also heard an awful rumor that some of the older students had caused the resignation of a previous teacher

by locking her out of the schoolhouse.

When Barton opened the door of her classroom, she found herself facing 40 expectant young faces, ranging in age from 4 to 13. Among them were four smirking bullies, all of them taller than their teacher. No one had told Barton what to do or how to prepare a lesson. How was she to begin? Her eyes fell upon the New Testament that lay on her desk. With sudden inspiration she reached for the book. She said:

> I asked them what they supposed the Saviour meant by saying that they must love their enemies and do good to them that hated and misused them.... This was a hard question and they hesitated, until at length a little bright-eyed girl, Emily, with great earnestness replied, "I think it means that you must be good to everybody, and mustn't quarrel nor make nobody feel bad, and I'm going to try." An ominous smile crept over the rather hard faces of my four lads, but my response was so prompt, and my approval so hearty, that it disappeared and they listened attentively but ventured no remarks.

Barton became an excellent and beloved teacher. County trustees later conferred upon her a badge of honor for having the best-disciplined classroom in the district. She continued to teach school in the area for more than a dozen years and was always in great demand. Then, driven by her own deep desire for further education, she enrolled at the Clinton Liberal Institute for female teachers in upstate New York.

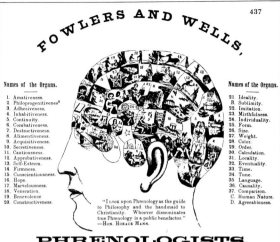

An advertisement for Fowlers and Wells, phrenologists. Lorenzo Niles Fowler paid Barton a visit in 1836.

At the Clinton Institute Barton's name was linked romantically with Samuel Ramsey, a divinity student at Hamilton College who later became one of Barton's aides in her Red Cross work. Their relationship came to an end over an unpaid debt. There were also stories of another suitor who went off to California during the gold rush in 1849 and succeeded in making his fortune. Rebuffed by Barton, he nevertheless deposited $10,000 to her account at a local bank. Barton initially refused to touch the money; it accumulated interest and was only put to use years later, in the service of humanitarian work.

Whether it was because Barton had a desire to fulfill herself through service to great causes, or because she had impossibly high ideals about marriage, she never wedded. Her nephew, Stephen E. Barton, wrote about her:

> My aunt said to me at one time that I must not think she had never known any experience of love. She said that she had had her romances and love affairs like other girls; but that in her young womanhood, though she thought of different men as possible lovers, no one of them measured up to her ideal of a husband. She said to me that she could think of herself with satisfaction as a wife and mother, but that on the whole she felt that she had been more useful to the world by being free from matrimonial ties.

Shortly after graduating from Clinton Barton was shattered by the sudden death of her mother. Captain Barton was staying with his son Stephen, and all of the sisters and brothers were married and had long since moved away from the old farm. So Barton decided to spend a few weeks with her good friend Mary Norton in Hightstown, New Jersey. Soon afterwards Barton found lodgings of her own and began to teach in nearby Bordentown.

The school in Bordentown where Barton taught was known as a "subscription school." In such a school, each student's family paid a fee toward

When Barton was 17 years old, she began her career as a schoolteacher at District School No. 9 in North Oxford.

the salary of the teacher. There was a state law requiring free public school education, but most wealthy people had no great desire to see the law enforced, and in many towns no free schools were available. The more well-to-do people of Bordentown would not think of sending their children to public, "pauper schools." They preferred to place their children in schools attended only by children whose parents could afford to pay for a teacher.

It soon became apparent to Barton that most of the children living in Bordentown did not, in fact, go to school. Great numbers of them clustered together on the street corners, idle, listless, and bored. Barton was curious about them and began to go out of her way to speak to them. They told her

that they could not go to school because they lacked money to pay for their education.

"Lady," one youngster told her, "there is no school for us. We would be glad to go if there was one."

That was enough for Barton. She marched directly to the office of Peter Suydam, the town postmaster, who also served as chairman of the school board. She told Suydam what she had observed and announced her intention to open up a free public school in Bordentown, which she would teach herself.

Suydam was shocked and dismayed. The boys, he told Barton, were renegades, "more fit for the penitentiary than school." A woman could not do anything with them. They would not

This teaching certificate, dated May 5, 1839, asserts that Barton "qualified as a Teacher of a Common School" in Oxford, Massachusetts.

Barton was officially certified to teach in Bordentown, New Jersey, after receiving this document on October 1, 1853.

Barton taught at this schoolhouse in Bordentown until illness forced her to resign from her post in early 1854.

go to school if they had the chance. He added that the respectable sentiment of the community would be against Barton and the action that she contemplated would bring disgrace upon her character.

Barton thanked him for the sincerity of his objections and his earnest desire to save her from what seemed an impossible undertaking. She then proceeded to point out to him that as an experienced teacher she had studied the character of the children on the streets and could not agree with his assessment of them. They filled her with intense pity, but not fear. Moreover, her own character, she assured him, was one that no village gossip could affect. Her only desire was to have the assistance of the board in opening a school in which outcast children would be taught. Furthermore, she would agree to teach them without pay, if necessary.

Suydam promised Barton that he would place her proposition before the school board, which was meeting the very next afternoon, and invited her to sit in on the board's deliberations. Barton heard many long discussions over the next few weeks. Despite the law upholding free public school education, several members of the board had deep misgivings about actually opening up a "pauper school." Finally, the board put the matter to a vote. The decision was unanimous. Clara Barton was allowed to have her school.

Soon afterward, in 1852, Barton became the mistress of a shabby old schoolhouse that the board had refitted for her use. On the first day there were only six pupils in the class, but the next day several more arrived, and the day after that even more. When the school reached an enrollment of 200, Barton asked her old friend Fannie Childs to come and help her teach. Suydam's wife, Jenny, also volunteered. Before long the children attending the fancy subscription schools had deserted them for Barton's classes, and the previously unpaid teachers were voted a salary by the board.

After one year the enrollment grew to 600, and a larger building was built in Bordentown to accommodate all the students. The board then decided that even though Barton had created the school, such an impressive institution was too large for a woman to run, and they appointed a young male principal. The young man was very jealous of Barton. He took every opportunity to criticize her and to side with the more unruly students against her. Although vigorous in fighting for the rights of others, Barton was not adept at defending herself. She soon came close to a nervous breakdown. Under the constant emotional strain she lost her voice, and, unable to speak above a whisper, in early 1854 resigned her position and left the school.

Barton, then 32 years old, was never to teach school again. Ill and exhausted, she left Bordentown and turned toward an unknown future.

A VIEW OF THE CITY OF WASHINGTON, D. C., FROM THE CAPITOL.

By the time Barton moved to Washington, D.C., in 1854, the growing city had been serving as the nation's capital for little more than a half century.

FOUR

War Comes to Washington

Barton recovered her health in the mild climate of Washington, D.C., welcoming the chance to stay with her sister Sally, who was living there with her husband. Thanks to the efforts of a distant relative, Massachusetts congressman Alexander De Witt, Barton was soon able to find employment and move to her own apartment. De Witt had introduced her to Charles Mason, who superintended the U.S. Patent Office. Mason had hired Barton to copy secret papers at 10 cents for every 100 words. Winning the esteem of her employer, Barton was asked to take charge of a confidential post from which information had previously been leaked. Explaining the promotion, she wrote:

> The secrecy of its papers had not been carefully guarded. I accepted and thus became as I believe the first woman who entered a public office in the Departments of Washington in her own name drawing the salary over on her

own signature. I was placed equal with the male clerks at $1,400 per year. This called for some criticism and no little denunciation on the part of those who foresaw dangerous precedents.

Some men did more than denounce Barton's presence. Walking through the hallways, she often had to endure rude stares and listen to unkind comments. Someone once spat tobacco juice at her. Finally, President Franklin Pierce and his secretary of the interior, Robert McClelland, made it their mission to get rid of women clerks because of what McClelland called "the obvious impropriety of the mixing of the sexes within the walls of a public office." Mason was forced to fight hard to keep Barton, especially after McClelland personally suggested to him that Barton work for Mason outside the Patent Office. Then in 1857 a new president, James Buchanan, was sworn in and Barton and Charles Mason, whose antislavery views ran counter to those of the Buchanan administration, were forced to resign.

Barton returned home to Massachusetts. For three years she supported herself by doing copy work for the Patent Office forwarded to her by post from Washington. Then she was suddenly summoned back to her old job. With a sense of jubilation, she welcomed a new administration under a president who shared her antislavery views: Abraham Lincoln, from the "free state" of Illinois.

Soon after Barton returned to Washington in 1860, she deliberately set about the task of making friends with people in high office. In the political atmosphere of Washington, she had come to realize that if she intended to keep her job she must make the right connections. She soon became a close personal friend of the powerful Senator Henry Wilson of Massachusetts.

As she had done in the past, Barton also took every available opportunity to sit in on debates in the Senate and in the House of Representatives. In this way she gained firsthand knowledge of the increasing tensions between northern and southern states, particularly over the issue of slavery. The legality of slavery was a bitter source of conflict among the states and among the territories seeking admission to the Union. But there were other issues dividing the country, such as whether to impose tariffs—to tax foreign goods

imported into the country. The industrial North wanted tariffs on imports in order to discourage foreign competition. The rural South, however, needed to import manufactured goods, and it naturally objected to this kind of tax.

In the spring of 1861 the state of South Carolina announced that it no longer wished to be part of the United States; it was seceding from the Union. Other southern states also threatened secession.

Barton was stunned along with the rest of the country when, on April 14, 1861, she learned that troops from South Carolina had attacked the federal forces holding Fort Sumter in Charleston harbor. After seceding from the Union, South Carolina had decided to lay claim to all U.S. properties within its borders.

Almost everyone in Washington knew what this news meant: the war that many people had been predicting was finally breaking out. President Lincoln would not surrender a fort of the United States to the state of South Carolina. Nor would he permit more states to secede from the Union.

Within hours after war had been declared, Barton saw the city of Washington transformed. Almost at once it began to fill with soldiers. Within days, the dusty, unpaved streets resounded with the sound of marching feet. Flags flew and drums rolled. The soldiers arrived every day by the trainload—often with no food and few supplies. They

Senator Henry Wilson became vice-president of the United States in 1873, serving under President Ulysses S. Grant. During the Civil War he was a general in the Union army.

came from every one of the free states. Food and lodgings had to be prepared, equipment and arms readied, training begun. As six more states seceded from the Union—Mississippi, Florida, Alabama, Georgia, Louisiana, and Texas—Lincoln sent out a call for 75,000 volunteers.

Barton visited the Washington Infirmary to see if she could be of any help. Perhaps someone there would be able to give her news about the arrival of any regiments from Massachusetts. There were sure to be former neighbors and students who might need assistance or supplies.

Yes, she discovered, the 6th Massa-chusetts Regiment had arrived, and yes, there were men from Worcester County. Barton found many of them in the infirmary, all suffering from bruises or broken bones. The men explained to her what had happened. While on their way to Washington they had stopped in Baltimore, Maryland, to change trains. Maryland was a border state between the North and the South, and a mob of Confederate sympathizers had attacked them. Four of their men had been killed and dozens more wounded. The mob had also stolen all their baggage. All that the men from Massachusetts had left were the clothes they were wearing. Unfortunately it was winter clothing—they were marching in long woolen underwear, clothing that would certainly be inappropriate for the hot spring and summer weather down south.

Barton learned that the men from the 6th Massachusetts Regiment were being quartered in the Senate chamber at the Capitol building. At once she hurried back to her own apartment and collected anything that she thought the men could use: needles and thread, buttons and pins, soap and tallow, stationery, and towels. She tore up her own sheets to make handkerchiefs. She loaded up a basket with pots and pans. She packed food and eating utensils. With her own money she bought summer underwear for the men.

It was Sunday, April 21, 1861, and the

The attack on Fort Sumter lasted for 36 hours and prompted President Abraham Lincoln to call for volunteers to fight the South, thus marking the start of the Civil War.

omnibuses were not running. Undaunted, she went out into the streets and hired five men to be her porters. Then, with her caravan in tow, she marched to the Capitol. A cheer went up as she entered the Senate chamber. The men had not eaten for many hours, nor had they known when they would be fed again. Hungrily, they devoured the food Barton had brought.

After the men had eaten, Barton had yet another surprise for them. From one of the baskets she pulled a copy of their hometown paper, *The Worcester Spy*. Mounting the speaker's rostrum, she read to the men the paper's entire account of the regiment's departure for the war.

In the days that followed, Barton took action to ensure that the men from Massachusetts would never again be without provisions. She advertised in the Worcester paper, stating that she would personally receive and distribute any provisions sent to the servicemen. She began a letter-writing campaign to friends, acquaintances, clergymen, and sewing circles in Massachusetts. The men also wrote home to their families about Barton. Before

Blood was first shed during the Civil War when Confederate mobs in Baltimore, Maryland, sought to prevent the 6th Massachusetts Regiment from arriving in Washington, D.C.

long, the women of Massachusetts responded. They sent blankets, clothing, canned foods, and preserves. They sent straw bedding for the men to sleep on. They sent salves, dressings, and medical supplies. Barton's one-room apartment was soon overflowing with boxes and crates piled up to the ceiling. In fact, there were so many packages that Barton finally got the army quartermaster, Major D. H. Rucker, to find a warehouse for them. Throughout 1862 Barton's stock of provisions never averaged less than five tons.

As the Civil War developed, the Southern leaders met in Montgomery, Alabama, and formed their own nation: the Confederate States of America. They elected Jefferson Davis as their president. Meanwhile, lacking methods of high-speed communication or transportation, the opposing armies groped to find each other.

News finally came of an impending battle at a place called Bull Run in Virginia. As though they were going to watch a sporting event, the wealthy ladies of Washington packed their lunches and followed the army on their carriages. They were soon sur-

rounded by a tide of Union soldiers who were fleeing in panic from the battlefront. The Union forces had been completely routed. The clash had left 500 soldiers dead and at least another 1,000 wounded.

Barton discovered that almost nothing had been done to prepare for the medical treatment of the soldiers. The wounded were brought to the docks of the Potomac River, where they lay untended in the open air until they could be brought into improvised hospital tents. Barton did whatever she could to help. She brought as many men as she possibly could back to her own lodgings, and she arranged a temporary leave from the Patent Office so that

A host of military passes were granted to Barton during the Civil War so she could attend to the wounded.

she could go to the docks to nurse the wounded.

As Barton continued to nurse the soldiers she became aware of an obvious fact: many of the wounded men died only because they had not been treated soon enough. Their injuries, left unbandaged for three or four days, had developed fatal infections or gangrene. Many men had simply bled to death. Often they had gone without food for days, and so they were faint from hunger. Barton realized that lives were needlessly being wasted because no one was treating the men at the battlefront.

Once again Barton began to write letters. She wrote to all of her contacts in Washington and to prominent officials in the War Department. She asked permission to bring her supplies to the men who were marching with General Ambrose Burnside's division. These were the men from Massachusetts, and Barton hoped to remain with them as a nurse. Yet even when she was making these appeals, Barton was struggling with her own self-doubt. She knew that what she was requesting from the army was something that was not considered "proper." In the mid-19th century people still believed that women lacked both the stamina and the courage to be anything but a nuisance at the front. And how would she be regarded by the soldiers?

Barton wrote in her journal:

I struggled long and hard with my sense of propriety—with the appalling fact that I was only a woman whispering in one ear and thundering in the other, the groans of suffering men dying like dogs, unfed and unsheltered, for the life of every institution which had protected and educated me! I said that I struggled with my sense of propriety and I say it with humiliation and shame.

While wrestling with these feelings Barton received word that her father, in his 88th year, was dying. At once she returned home to nurse him. Barton told him about her misgivings. There are many fathers who would have discouraged their daughters from undertaking a mission as dangerous as going to the front, but Captain Barton reassured his daughter. "I know soldiers," he said, "and they will respect you and your errand." Then he gave her his Masonic emblem—a symbol of his membership in an international secret fraternal society—and assured her that those who belonged to this brotherhood would furnish her with assistance and protection.

On the day of Captain Barton's funeral Barton received the letter for which she had prayed:

Miss C. H. Barton has permission to go upon the sick transports in any direction—for the purpose of distributing comforts for the sick and wounded—of nursing them, always subject to the direction of the surgeon in charge.

It was signed by William A. Hammond, surgeon general of the United States.

The U.S. Sanitary Commission was the main organization for nursing wounded soldiers during the Civil War. The organization was made up of volunteers such as the ones shown here.

FIVE

The Battlefield Nurse

At the time of the outbreak of the Civil War the first nursing school had not yet opened its doors, nor would it do so for another dozen years. Those who nursed the wounded, including Barton, learned their skills on the job. Although women had always undertaken the task of nursing the wounded in battle, they did so well behind the lines.

Nursing during the Civil War was administered mainly by an organization called the U.S. Sanitary Commission. Its members included thousands of volunteers who gathered supplies, made bandages and clothing, and staffed military hospitals with nurses. During the war the Sanitary Commission was administered by the Reverend Henry Bellows and the able Dorothea Dix, who had won fame with her reforms for treating the mentally ill. Other nursing organizations included Soldiers Aid societies and the spiritually-oriented Christian Commission. Female nurses, however, were not sent to the front, nor were army surgeons desirous of their assistance. Barton would change all that.

On Sunday, August 31, 1862, the Second Battle of Bull Run was fought in Fairfax, Virginia. Barton was sitting in the boxcar of an army train bound for the battlefront. She had already been initiated into battlefield service several weeks before at Cedar Mountain in Virginia. Arriving there by herself on a mule-drawn wagon, she had come to the rescue of Brigade Surgeon James I. Dunn, who was out of medical supplies. Dunn had called her "the Angel of the Battlefield," a name that would follow her throughout the war. It would not be the last time that Barton

A group of drawings published in Harper's Weekly *in 1862 let the nation know that its Northern women were actively involved in the war effort.*

and Dunn would meet, and the overworked surgeon would often have cause to sing her praises.

Despite the restriction against women on the battlefield, Barton somehow managed to gain clearance for three other female volunteers to accompany her to Bull Run: Almira Fales, Ada Morrell, and Lydie Haskell. There were no seats and no windows in the boxcar, and the women sat in almost total darkness, propped up against stacks of boxes, crates, and barrels. Only the sound of artillery in the distance told them they were nearing the battlefront.

At mid-morning the train chugged to a stop. Several soldiers appeared astonished to see four women included with the freight. Since there were no steps down to the platform, the soldiers helped each woman to the ground while other men climbed into the car and began to unload boxes onto the platform.

The women gazed for the first time at the incredible spectacle before them. Stretched out on the hillside as far as the eye could see were the bloody and mangled bodies of the wounded. At the edges of the wooded field army wagons were unloading still more bodies. Within 15 minutes the

Now regarded as one of the most capable men ever to govern the country, Abraham Lincoln was elected to the presidency in 1860 despite failing to receive a majority of the popular vote.

This 1861 woodcut depicts a nursing scene in a Washington hospital.

women had begun to work. Fires were made and two kettles of water were set to boil, one for soup and the other for washing wounds. The boxes of food and dressings were unwrapped.

Then came a crisis. Barton was dismayed to learn that there were no eating utensils. She quickly took stock of the provisions: there were several water buckets, five tin cups, a stew pan, a tin dish, three plates, and four bread knives for 3,000 men. She realized that there was only one thing to do. After each jar of preserves and container of food they had brought had been used up, it was converted into a dish.

Far into the night the women baked bread, ladled out soup, gave out shirts to clothe the bodies, dressed wounds, and jotted down the names of the injured so that their families could be notified. Passing out soup or bread soaked in wine, Barton was moved to see some of the men shed tears. Many had not eaten for several days.

Hard upon the Second Battle of Bull Run came the battles of Fairfax Court House and Chantilly, both in Virginia. At Chantilly Barton bound the mangled arm of a former pupil, Charley Hamilton; her one brief respite in two sleepless nights was the hour she spent comforting Hugh Johnson. Then, on the third night of the battle at Chantilly, came thunder, lightning, and, finally, torrents of rain. Thunder vied with the volleys of the cannon and the rain blasted like gunshot at the earth. Yet the army wagons kept on arriving, bringing in more dead and wounded. Long after her assistants had given up, Barton kept on working. Finally, she felt she could no longer stay awake and sought the shelter of her army tent. She fell several times on the way from sheer exhaustion.

Entering her little tent at last, Barton found herself almost knee-deep in water—the entire floor of the tent was a swirling stream. But Barton was too exhausted to care. She sat down in the water, supported by some boxes, and fell asleep. Of this episode, she wrote:

> I remember myself sitting on the ground, upheld by my left arm, my head resting on my hand, impelled by an

Women often met in groups to prepare supplies for the Civil War troops.

almost uncontrollable desire to lie completely down and prevented by the certain conviction that if I did, water would flow into my ears.

She allowed herself to sleep only for two hours. Then she wrung out her dress and her hair and returned to work. Seeing the wounded being loaded onto a train, Barton realized that none of these soldiers would be fed for at least 24 hours—until the train reached Washington. Approaching one of the officers, she asked that the wag-

In 1861 Robert E. Lee was offered, but refused, command of the Union armies. Appointed to command the Confederate forces in June 1862, General Lee proved to be an expert leader and strategist.

ons bringing in the wounded be stopped at a certain checkpoint. And no man should be moved beyond that point until he had been fed. The officer at once saw the reasonableness of Barton's request.

As she supervised the feeding of the wounded, a soldier galloped up with bad news. Union General Philip Kearny had been slain, and his demoralized followers were retreating, with the enemy in full pursuit. Barton later recorded the messenger's words in her journal:

> "Miss Barton, can you ride?"
> "Yes, sir," I replied.
> "But you have no lady's saddle—could you ride mine?"
> "Yes, sir, or without it, if you have a blanket and surcingle [a belt or girth]."
> "Then you can risk another hour," he exclaimed, and galloped off.
> At four he returned at breakneck speed, and, leaping from his horse said, "Now is your time. The enemy is already breaking over the hills. Try the train. It will go through, unless they have flanked and cut the bridge a mile above us. In that case I've a reserve horse for you and you must take your chances to escape across the country."

In a matter of minutes Barton was on the train, but so was every one of her patients. The conductor took a torch and set fire to the station so that it would not fall into enemy hands. As the train pulled away and rounded a bend in the track, Barton could see the station all ablaze and the rebel cavalry galloping down the hill.

A daring and controversial soldier, General Ulysses S. Grant won a number of big victories before Lincoln appointed him commander of all the Union armies in early 1864.

President Abraham Lincoln addresses some of his men at Antietam Creek, in Maryland, where the Confederates' first attempt to advance into the North was repulsed.

SIX

Antietam

In September 1862, with the war showing no sign of abating, Barton found herself in another mule-drawn wagon, clopping along the dusty roads of Maryland as part of a 10-mile-long Union army caravan. This time she had not been permitted to take along female companions. Her assistants were five soldiers.

The army was heading toward the city of Sharpsburg, Maryland. During the 80-mile trip, Barton busied herself by cutting loaves of bread and passing them out to the haggard, famished soldiers who marched along on foot beside the wagons. At every village they passed through she got out and bought more bread, spending her own money.

Barton was worried, since the hospital supplies were in the rear of the caravan, well behind the cannon, the ammunition, food, and clothing. If there was to be a battle, it would be three days at the very least before medical supplies would reach the battlefront. The position of the wagons, moreover, could not be altered. It was "as fixed," Barton wrote, "as the position of the planets."

There was only one thing to do. At 1 A.M., when the army had camped for the night and everyone was sleeping, Barton asked her driver to harness up the mules. If the hospital supply wagon set out before the camp awakened it could eventually make its way to the front of the caravan.

By daybreak the wagon had caught up with the cannon. Nightfall brought the wagon to General Ambrose Burnside's corps. There they found the two opposing armies camped on either side of Antietam Creek. In the morning the sun rose over the Blue Ridge Mountains and a bugle sang the clarion call to battle.

The successful capture of this bridge at Antietam Creek by Union General Ambrose Burnside and his men helped to stop the advance of Southern troops.

Not sure where to go, Barton listened carefully. To the right of the camp, the firing was the thickest—that was where the aid would be most needed. Guided by the gunfire, Barton and her assistants drove their wagon into the cover of a cornfield, where the shells were whistling loudly overhead. Fighting their way through the corn jungle, the group soon found itself at the edge of a large clearing. There, spread out in every direction around a barn, were at least 300 wounded men. Many were badly injured and crying out in pain, but no one seemed to be taking care of them. Where were the doctors? Bar-

ton wondered. Surely they must be nearby.

Suddenly, she saw a little path winding through the cornfield and guessed that it led to a house where the surgeons must be working. While her assistants went to work treating the wounded, she gathered up armfuls of stimulants and dressings and made her way alone along the path.

The path led her to the doorway of an old farmhouse, where Barton saw that she had guessed correctly. On the house's wide porch stood four operating tables. Upon each table lay an unconscious form, and working over

The combined death toll for the North and the South at the Battle of Antietam was 26,000.

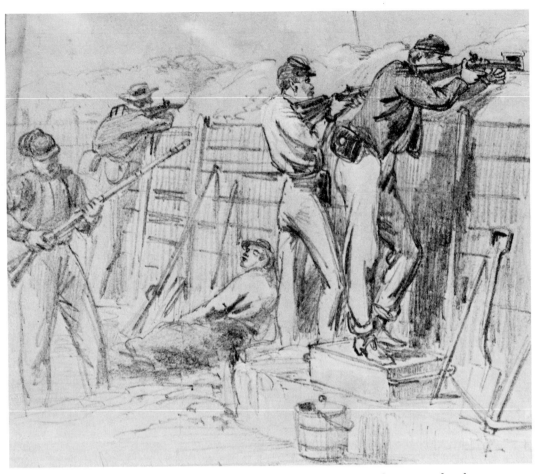

Fighting from a trench meant being bound to a fixed position. It often proved to be as dangerous as fighting in an open field.

each body was a surgeon. Barton found herself face to face with Brigade Surgeon Dunn. For a moment he was speechless; then he threw up his hands. "God has indeed remembered us," the doctor said. He then asked her:

"How did you get from Virginia so soon? And again to supply our necessities! And they are terrible. We have nothing but our instruments and the little chloroform we brought in our pockets. We have not a bandage, rag, lint or string, and all these shell-wounded men bleeding to death."

Gazing at the men on the tables, Barton saw what the surgeons had been using for dressings—the green husks of corn! Laying down her bandages on each table, she thought that linen had never looked so white.

The need for able-bodied soldiers eventually became so great that both sides ultimately sought to enlist any man who was physically capable of combat.

Three times during that day the Battle of Antietam was contested, lost, and won. Each time hundreds of newly wounded men were brought to the farmhouse's already crowded rooms. The artillery smoke became so thick it obscured the soldiers' sight. The sulfur from gunshot parched their lips till they bled, and the roar of the cannon thundered in their ears.

A man lying on the ground asked for a drink. Barton raised his head up with her right hand to give it to him. Just at that moment a bullet sped between them, tearing a hole in her sleeve. The man she had been holding fell back dead.

Barton said of this scene:

The patient endurance of these men was most astonishing. As many as could

51

be were carried into the barn, as a slight protection against random shot. Just outside the door lay a man wounded in the face, the ball having entered the lower maxillary on the left side and lodged among the bones of the right cheek. His imploring look drew me to him, when, placing his finger upon the sharp protuberance he said, "Lady, will you tell me what this is that burns so?" I replied it must be a ball. . . .

"It is terribly painful," he said. "Won't you take it out?" I said I would go to the tables for a surgeon. "No! No!" he said, catching my dress. "They cannot come to me. I must wait my turn, for this is a little wound. You can get the ball. There is a knife in your pocket. Please take the ball out for me."

Barton was frightened. She had never operated on a man. She told him she would hurt him too much.

> He looked up, with as nearly a smile as such a mangled face could assume, saying, "You cannot hurt me, dear lady. I can endure any pain that your hands can create."

Barton drew out her pocket knife. Just then, a stalwart sergeant who lay nearby and who had been wounded in the fleshy part of his thigh crawled along the ground and joined them. Taking his fellow soldier's head firmly in his hands, the sergeant held it while Barton extracted the musket ball.

In the middle of the afternoon a Sergeant Fields, one of 30 additional assistants Barton had managed to gather, came to deliver some most unwelcome news. The last loaf of bread in their stores had been cut, and there was nothing to feed the wounded. What should they do now?

Barton remembered that there were 12 boxes of wine packed with her provisions. She instructed the soldiers to give it to the men. Sergeant Fields opened the first box and cried out. A miracle had happened! The wine had been packed not in sawdust but in cornmeal! All 12 boxes were pried open—three were found to have been packed with the precious meal. The farmhouse had six big kettles, which Barton filled with water and set to boiling. She was soon busy making gruel.

Then another idea occurred to her. Perhaps there were some provisions stored in the cellar. Calling several of her assistants, she had them force open the door that barred the stairs. Sure enough, down in the cool dampness of the cellar they found three barrels of flour and a bag of salt. All bore the label of the Confederate army. Barton felt as though she had discovered gold.

Assured now that the wounded would be fed, Barton made her way back to the barn and continued to minister to the wounded. Several hours later, as dusk was falling, she decided to walk back to the farmhouse to see if Dr. Dunn had need of her. She described the encounter that ensued:

> I went to the house and found the surgeon in charge, sitting alone beside a table, upon which he rested his elbow, apparently meditating upon a bit of

Troops from the North and the South exchange fire while only yards apart.

tallow candle which flickered in the center. Approaching carefully, I said, "You are tired, Doctor."

He started up with a look almost savage. "Tired! Yes, I am tired, tired of such heartlessness, such carelessness!" Turning full upon me, he continued: "Think of the condition of things. Here are at least one thousand wounded men, terribly wounded. Five hundred of whom cannot live till daylight without attention. That two inches of candle is all I have or can get. What can I do? How can I endure it?"

I took him by the arm, and, leading him to the door, pointed in the direction of the barn where the lanterns glistened like stars among the waving corn. "What is that?" he exclaimed. "The barn is lighted," I said. "And the house will be directly." "Who did it?" "I, Doctor." "Where did you get them?" "Brought them with me." "How many have you?" "All you want—four boxes."

Dr. Dunn looked at Barton as if he was waking from a dream, then his eyes filled with respect. He did not speak, nor were words necessary.

In December 1862 Union General Ambrose Burnside commanded 114,000 men at the Battle of Fredericksburg. Despite his large army, he failed to come away with a victory.

SEVEN

Fredericksburg and Spotsylvania

Barton had learned much in her first battles. She now knew that when she traveled with the army she must station her wagon just behind the guns. That way she could arrive at the battlefront at the earliest possible moment. She had also made it her business to find informers who could tell her when and where a new battle was taking place.

Ill with exhaustion from the Battle of Antietam, Barton was convalescing in Washington when word reached her that she was needed in Virginia. With scarcely two weeks' rest she was soon on her way, this time fully stocked by the army quartermaster, Major D. H. Rucker, who gave Barton six wagonloads of supplies and an ambulance, each drawn by a team of six mules. Placed under her command were seven stout mule drivers who were not

soldiers but civilians employed by the government to deliver army goods.

The moment Barton looked at their faces she knew there would be trouble. Veterans in their line of work, they were rough, unmannerly men who worked with mules—they were not about to be led by a woman. No sooner had they caught up with the Union army as it crossed the Potomac River near Harper's Ferry, West Virginia, than the men mutinied and said they would not cross. Barton told them plainly that if they did not wish to go forward they would be dismissed and replaced by soldiers. Grumbling angrily, they obeyed her order. She then told them to drive on only until dusk, but once again they spitefully defied her, driving on far into the night. At last they tired of their little game, and they stopped to camp beside an open field.

The many assaults by the North during the Battle of Fredericksburg often ended with little position gained and many lives lost.

luminating their faces. They seemed to her like a band of pirates. Nervously, she invited them to sit down and warm themselves by the fire. There was silence at first; then the leader, whose name was George, stepped forward.

"No, thank you," George replied. "We didn't come to warm us, we are used to the cold. But ... we come to tell you that we are ashamed of ourselves. . . . The truth is, in the first place we didn't want to come. There's fighting ahead and we've seen enough of that ... and then we never seen a train under the charge of a woman before and we couldn't understand it and we didn't like it. And we thought we'd break it up, and we've been mean and contrary all day, and said a good many hard things and you've treated us like gentlemen. We hadn't no right to expect that supper you gave us—a better meal than we've had in two years. And you've been as polite to us as we'd been the General and his staff, and it makes us ashamed. And we've come to ask your forgiveness. We shan't trouble you no more."

While the men were busy tending their mules Barton kindled a fire and prepared supper. Barton knew that the men carried few provisions with them, mainly hard crackers and dried meat. So she took food from her own supplies and made them the best dinner that she could. Then she spread a white cloth on the ground and called the men to supper. When they were seated, she sat and ate with them, chatting as if nothing were the matter.

The men spoke very little but devoured the food. Afterward, they melted away into the night. Left alone, Barton scraped the plates and began to wash the dishes. Suddenly, the men reappeared out of the darkness. She watched them come toward her, the glowing red embers of the campfire il-

Barton forgave them at once with good cheer. Stirring their patriotic sentiment, she reminded them that their country needed them. She promised that she would share in their fortunes. "When you are hungry and supperless," she told them, "I will be too. If harm befalls you, I will care for you: if sick, I will nurse you and under all circumstances, I will treat you like gentlemen."

The men listened silently, although a few of them had tears glistening in

Bodies lie in a field after the Battle of Gettysburg. The North's triumph here on July 1–3, 1863, marked a major turning point of the war.

their eyes. Finally, they all withdrew—except for George, who went to the wagon in which Barton slept and arranged the quilts on her bed. Then he lifted Barton into the wagon and buckled the flap of the canvas down securely. After carefully putting out the campfire, he lay down to sleep nearby on the ground.

In December 1862 Barton learned that the two armies were massing near Virginia's Rappahannock River. The Southern troops, under General Robert E. Lee, were posted upon the south

bank of the river near the city of Fredericksburg. On the north bank, Union General Ambrose Burnside was hoping to succeed at a frontal attack by constructing rope bridges across the water.

Arriving at Burnside's camp, Barton stationed herself at Lacy House, one of the area's larger mansions. Soon she was hard at work organizing a kitchen and supervising the nursing of hundreds of wounded, who soon covered the floor of every room and even had to be placed on available shelves.

President Lincoln prepares to give his landmark address on democracy at the Gettysburg military cemetery on November 19, 1863.

The following day a courier arrived at the camp with a bloodstained message for Barton from Dr. Clarence Cutter, the medical director of the 9th Army Corps. Dr. Cutter had set up another hospital across the river, where Union soldiers were fighting the rebels. "Come to me," the note pleaded. "Your place is here."

The mule drivers, who two months earlier had given Barton such trouble, now turned pale at the thought that Barton meant to cross the Rappahannock. The fighting there was at its thickest, and Burnside's men had been turned back time and again as they sought to cross the bridges. One of the drivers offered to go in her place. Barton told him that he could not take her place, but that he might go with her if he liked. Soon they were crossing one of the rope bridges, swaying and rocking as gunshot exploded around them.

On the opposite shore a Union officer stepped to Barton's side to assist her. A shell flew between them, taking away a portion of Barton's dress. Nearly a half hour later the same officer was brought to her—dead.

Arriving in Fredericksburg, Barton realized that the entire town had become a battlefield. Fighting was going on in the streets, and every building was being used as a fortress. Dead soldiers were lying everywhere. The churches and the schools, as well as many houses, had all been converted into hospitals, and their yards were filled with the wounded and the dying.

As she moved among the soldiers, Barton saw the provost marshal, General Patrick, riding toward her. Mistaking her for one of the residents of the city, he bent down from his saddle and said to her in a gentle, kindly voice, "You are alone and in great danger, Madam. Do you want protection?"

"Thank you very much," Barton replied. "But I believe I'm the best protected woman in the United States."

Several soldiers nearby heard her words. "That's so, that's so," they cried.

And they sent up a cheer that echoed through the ranks.

Taking in the situation, the general bowed his head. "I believe you are right, Madam," he said with a smile. Without another word he galloped off.

Toward dusk, the Union army was forced to retreat back across the river with the wounded. Included among these wounded were many Confederate soldiers, some of whom had lain for several days in the snow and had to be hacked free from it with axes. Barton had a clearing made in the snow and built several large fires around which she gently placed the wounded. Then she had the men wrapped in blankets. Finally, an old chimney was torn down. The bricks were fireheated and then placed around the men. A good meal left most of them sleeping comfortably until morning.

After taking a brief rest in Washington, Barton went to Port Royal, near Charleston, South Carolina, where her brother David was quartermaster. Barton also hoped to hear news of her brother Stephen, who had moved to North Carolina before the war and had not been heard from since. Meanwhile, the Union army attacked Charleston and held the city under siege for eight months. There were also battles fought on nearby islands. And with men stricken with tropical diseases, Barton never found herself short of work.

A terrible battle was being fought near Fredericksburg, at a place called Spotsylvania. Even as battle-hardened as she was, Barton could report, "I saw many things that I did not wish to see and I pray God I may never see again."

What Barton saw were hundreds of army wagons mired hopelessly in a lake of red mud. The wagons were full

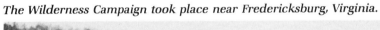
The Wilderness Campaign took place near Fredericksburg, Virginia.

of bleeding, wounded men waiting to be shipped to Washington. The wagons extended so far down the Wilderness Road that Barton could not find the last of them. Every animal was sunk in mud up to its knees, and not a wheel of a wagon could be seen. To make matters worse, nobody seemed to know what to do. There was mass confusion.

Barton had given out the last of her food when a young clergyman offered her a large quantity of crackers for the soldiers. Barton proceeded to boil a big kettle of coffee, and armed with coffee and crackers, she and the clergyman moved down a grassy slope to where the dry land joined the mud. Barton would remember the "expression of consternation and dismay depicted in every feature of his fine face" as the clergyman asked her how they were to get to the men. "There is no way to but to walk," answered Barton. And she strode into the waist-high mud.

Afterward, Barton went into an old hotel where a bloody floor was covered with gaunt, starving bodies. As she walked by, the soldiers pleaded for food and drink, but Barton had nothing left to give them. Her mind filled with horror, she stumbled out into the

Wounded Union soldiers wait for aid to arrive at Fredericksburg.

street. Nearby, an army captain was telling a fellow officer that the "refined people of Fredericksburg" should not have to open up their homes to "these dirty, lousy, common soldiers." Enraged at his callousness, Barton commandeered a light army wagon and galloped at full speed toward a nearby landing, where she boarded a steam tug for Washington. Once there, she sent for her friend, Senator Henry Wilson.

The chairman of the Senate Military Committee, Wilson listened to Barton describe what she had seen. Her story made his face turn white and made him shake with anger. That same night he summoned the War Department and related Barton's story. The men at the War Department did not believe him, however, for no report of unusual suffering had reached them. Therefore, the story could not possibly be true.

In her journal, Barton recorded what happened next:

> It was then that Wilson proved my confidence in his firmness was not misplaced as, facing his doubters he replied: "One of two things will have to be done—either you will send someone tonight with the power to investigate and correct the abuses of our wounded men . . . or the Senate will send someone tomorrow."

At 2 A.M. the next morning the quartermaster general and his staff left to investigate Barton's story. By morning the wounded were being fed and housed.

The battle at Spotsylvania lasted for 12 days. The worst day of the long battle left 12,000 men dead.

Matthew Brady, one of the most noted photographers in the 19th century, took this portrait of Barton during the Civil War.

EIGHT

Searching for the Missing

It was 1865, and the war was in its fourth year. Despite an initial string of victories, the South was losing the war. The Union army had blockaded the South's seaports, and many Southerners were starving. Union General William Tecumseh Sherman had contributed to this condition by marching through Georgia in November and December of 1864, burning everything in his path. Lincoln's Emancipation Proclamation had prompted former slaves to leave their owners and flock to the Union cause. Out west, Union General Ulysses S. Grant was winning battle after battle.

During this time, Barton found herself in an executive position. She had been appointed superintendent of nurses for the Army of the James under General Benjamin F. Butler. Stationed at Point of Rocks, on a former plantation near Petersburg, Virginia, it was her job to organize hospitals and their staffs and to tend to their daily administration. As usual, Barton worked without pay, often using her own funds to supply needed items and to obtain special home-style delicacies for her patients.

One day a letter was brought to Barton from her brother Stephen in North Carolina. He had been taken prisoner by the Union army. Ill and unconscious when he was captured, he had been mistreated by the soldiers and was now languishing in a Yankee prison. With the help of her superior, General Butler, Barton at once had Stephen sent to her. Quarters were found for him in an old slaves' cabin that stood on the plantation where she was working. Although Barton nursed Stephen for many months, he did not recover and died in March 1865. On April 9 Confederate General Robert E. Lee sur-

President Lincoln's assassination on April 15, 1865, occurred less than a month after the fighting of the Civil War had stopped.

rendered at Appomattox, Virginia, bringing the Civil War to a close.

During the spring of 1865, Barton plunged into political causes. Befriending ex-slave leaders such as Frederick Douglass and suffragists such as Susan B. Anthony, she lobbied for the rights of ex-slaves and labored to bring women the right to vote. When time permitted, she also tried to answer the many letters that came to her daily from the families of missing soldiers. Barton was by now very well known, and many people wrote to her on the chance that she had nursed someone they loved.

It was while she was answering some of these letters that Barton was struck by a new idea. The War Department had no organization for tracing missing soldiers. Why not organize such a search herself?

Barton sat down and wrote a letter to President Lincoln, asking for the authority to act as general correspondent at Annapolis, Maryland, for those seeking information about the missing. Lincoln granted her the authority she requested in what was to be one of his final acts. Only days later, on April 14, 1865, he was assassinated in a Washington theater by the actor John Wilkes Booth. Since the president's death took place before any arrangement could be made to fund her work, Barton had once again to rely on her own money.

Barton took up residence in an army tent at Annapolis and set up her "Office

of Correspondence with Friends of the Missing Men of the U.S. Army." Using her famous gift for organization she sorted the names of the men who were missing by state. These lists were published in newspapers all over the country. Soon letters began to pour in, at least 100 a day. Sometimes Barton was able to tell a wife or mother that her loved one would be returning home. At other times she had to tell a family that their loved one had died. Yet there were still thousands of men unaccounted for no matter how hard Barton worked.

One day, Barton received a visit from

A notice announces one of Barton's many lectures.

Barton saw to it that the Confederate prison at Andersonville, Georgia, was turned into a national cemetery.

a young man from Connecticut named Dorence Atwater. He told Barton that he had been a prisoner at Andersonville, the South's infamous prison camp in Georgia. Conditions at this camp had been so brutal that Yankee prisoners had died there by the thousands. All of them had been buried in shallow graves, under markers that bore only code numbers, not names.

Atwater told Barton that he knew the names of the men buried in those graves. Since he had excellent penmanship, the Confederate officers had used him to keep a tally of all the Yankee prisoners who had died. In addition to making the list of names, Atwater had kept track of the order of the graves. When Barton asked how he had managed to keep this list, Atwater told her that he had secretly made a copy of it and sewed it into the lining of his coat.

Barton could hardly believe this

stroke of good fortune. There were 13,000 names on Atwater's list, and now their families could be notified. Using her political connections, Barton saw to it that the Andersonville camp was turned into a national cemetery. Visiting the camp with Atwater, she supervised the needed work herself. The dead were reinterred in deep graves, and a fresh marker bearing the name of the soldier who lay beneath was placed on each gravesite.

Barton worked at locating the missing for nearly four years and helped to find more than 22,000 soldiers. During this time the bureau for finding missing men that she had established became an indispensable agency of the U.S. government. Without daily reference to Barton's records, the government would have been unable to settle accounts for such things as back pay and soldiers' pensions. Congress also reimbursed Barton for the $15,000 of her own money that she had spent, and it voted new money for her bureau.

Long before Congress reimbursed her, however, Barton had exhausted all of her own funds. In 1866, in order to earn money to continue her work, she was forced to undertake a lecture tour. Describing her life and work during the war, she found herself much in demand as a speaker. She traveled all over the North and West, often billed with such leading authors as Ralph Waldo Emerson and Mark Twain. Between 1867 and 1868 alone she delivered 300 lectures.

However, the stress of Barton's schedule eventually took its toll. One evening in 1868, when she was about to begin a lecture at the opera house in Portland, Maine, she opened her mouth, but could not speak. Just as at school in Bordentown so many years earlier, Barton had lost her voice. She folded her papers and walked off the stage. Ill and once more on the verge of a nervous breakdown, she realized that it was time to close another chapter in her life.

The signing of the Treaty of Geneva took place on August 22, 1864, and set the stage for the emergence of the International Red Cross.

NINE

European Adventures

Barton's doctor insisted that she take a long rest. Only then could she hope to recover her health. He suggested that she go abroad for a few years, and she agreed.

During the Civil War Barton had once nursed a young Swiss soldier named Jules Golay. Later on, he had assisted her with her efforts to locate the missing. Learning that Barton meant to travel abroad, he notified his parents, who invited Barton to stay with them in Switzerland. After visiting several other countries she joined the Golays in Geneva, Switzerland. It was there that Dr. Louis Appia of the Red Cross found her.

Dr. Appia realized he was grasping at straws. He had little hope that Barton could help his organization but thought it worth a try. In September 1869, a month after Barton's arrival in Geneva, Dr. Appia, accompanied by several other distinguished-looking citizens, paid her a visit. The men told Barton that they were members of the International Committee of Geneva—otherwise known as the Red Cross.

Barton was surprised to discover that Dr. Appia, the president of this organization, knew all about her work during the Civil War. He told her that the Red Cross was devoted to relieving just the kind of suffering she had seen. What Appia wanted Barton to tell him—and this was the prime reason for his visit—was why the United States had three times refused to join his organization.

Barton did not know the answer. She had never heard of the Red Cross; naturally, she wanted to learn all about it. So Dr. Appia explained to her how the organization had been created by Jean-Henri Dunant. For the first time in her life Barton heard about another battle-

Dr. Louis Appia was the first to inform Barton of the existence of the International Red Cross.

Before founding the International Red Cross, Jean-Henri Dunant was part of the group that established the Young Men's Christian Association (YMCA).

field nurse who had witnessed the same horrors she had seen: the starvation, the needless suffering, the confusion.

A wealthy Swiss industrialist, Dunant had gone to Italy in 1859 on business. While there he witnessed a battle between the Austrians and an alliance of French and Italian soldiers. Called the Battle of Solferino, it is considered by some historians to have been one of the bloodiest clashes of the 19th century. It left 40,000 people dead or wounded.

Belonging to a family with a long-

standing tradition of public service, Dunant nursed the wounded of that battle and also organized relief for them. He later wrote about his wartime experiences in a book called *A Memory of Solferino*. In this book Dunant not only described the misery he had witnessed but also proposed a solution. Would it not be possible, he asked, to form relief organizations during a time of peace so that when war broke out, the wounded could be cared for by qualified volunteers? Dunant suggested that these volunteers, as well as the wounded, their hospitals, convey-

Dunant decided to found the International Red Cross after witnessing the bloody Battle of Solferino in northern Italy.

ances, and supplies, be considered neutral and safe from attack.

The book created an immediate sensation when it was published in 1862. In particular, it sparked the imagination of a Swiss philanthropist named Gustave Moynier. The president of a distinguished group of scholars, the Society for Public Benefit, Moynier invited Dunant to work with his society to promote the proposal for an international relief organization. Dunant agreed, and together they created a special task force that called itself the Committee of Five. This committee,

which also included Dr. Appia, soon set about marshalling support for Dunant's ideas among the various heads of state in Europe.

In 1863 a conference was held in Geneva that was attended by delegates from 16 nations. At this conference formal recognition was given to the need for a relief organization such as that proposed by Dunant and Moynier. The delegates agreed that an international emblem should be chosen for this organization, to be used by all member nations. Since the Committee of Five had been organized in Geneva, the delegates decided to honor the Swiss flag, which has a white cross on a field of red; reversing the colors, they created the emblem of the Red Cross.

Dr. Appia explained to Barton that at a second conference an agreement known as the Geneva Convention of 1864 for the Amelioration of the Condition of the Wounded and Sick of Armies in the Field, or the Treaty of Geneva, had been signed by 12 of the 16 nations. This treaty, which set up the machinery of the International Red Cross, not only adapted Dunant's ideas on the medical care of the wounded but also set forth new and humane rules for the treatment of civilians and prisoners of war.

Red Cross field hospitals such as this one were set up during the Franco-Prussian War.

Attending the Geneva meeting were two representatives from the United States: George C. Fogg, the U.S. ambassador to Switzerland, and Charles S. Bowles, European agent for the U.S. Sanitary Commission. Yet the representatives of the American government refused to sign the treaty. During the five years since the Geneva Convention

This Red Cross ambulance group provided aid when the Germans laid siege to Paris during the Franco-Prussian War.

Wounded soldiers are brought to Paris as the French are forced to retreat during the Franco-Prussian War.

had been drafted, many other nations had joined the Red Cross. However, the United States still had not.

Barton could not understand why her government had refused to join such a worthwhile organization. She could only suppose that bureaucracy was to blame, or that the purpose of the organization had been misunderstood. Commenting on her dismay she wrote:

Not a civilized people in the world but ourselves missing, and I saw Greece, Spain and Turkey there. I began to fear that in the eyes of the rest of mankind we could not be far from barbarians. This reflection did not furnish a stimulating food for national pride. I grew more and more ashamed.

As Dr. Appia had hoped, Barton promised the Committee of Five that she would try to help them. But for the time being there was nothing she could do. She was ill, and her doctors had ordered her to take three years of rest. Within months, however, an event occurred that raised Barton from her sickbed and bound her destiny to that of the Red Cross: the outbreak of the Franco-Prussian War.

This war marked the first time that two countries that had signed the Treaty of Geneva—Germany and France—were engaged in battle. The main cause of the war was the pressure placed on France when Germany's chancellor, Otto von Bismarck, sought to have a member of the German imperial family gain ascension to the throne in Spain. Fearful of Bismarck's expansionist designs, Napoleon III of France viewed the German chancellor's move as a threat to his own country and abruptly declared war on Germany.

Within hours following the declaration of war, Barton received a visit from Grand Duchess Louise of Baden, daughter of King Wilhelm I of Prussia. The petite, dark-haired grand duchess was a patron of the Red Cross, and she wanted Barton to organize relief for the impending conflict.

Barton quickly forgot all about her illness. Throughout her lifetime she seemed to stage the most miraculous recoveries when the battlefield called her. Within days she was on her way to the city of Basel, Switzerland. Situated on a high bluff overlooking the Rhine River, Basel had been chosen by the Germans and the French as a Red Cross center. While helping to make bandages there, Barton observed with growing admiration what the Red Cross was able to accomplish.

French emperor Napoleon III declared war on Prussia on July 19, 1870, but was unable to stop the unification of the Prussian states into the German Empire.

I saw ... the work of these Red Cross societies in the field accomplishing in four months under this systematic organization what we had failed to accomplish in four years without it—no mistakes, no needless suffering, no starving, no lack of care, no waste, no confusion, but order, plenty, cleanliness and comfort wherever that little flag made its way—a whole continent marshalled under the banner of the Red Cross.

Finding the work at Basel too tame for her liking Barton traveled to Mulhouse, across the border in France. She was interested in nursing the wounded, and Mulhouse was supposedly near the fighting. Acting as Barton's interpreter for the journey was a tall, gentle, fair-haired young art student named Antoinette Margot. Assigned to Barton by the Red Cross, she and Barton were to become close and lifelong friends.

The two women discovered that they were not needed in Mulhouse, and so they continued on to Strasbourg, France, hoping that the American consul there could tell them how to get to the battlefront. In Strasbourg Barton was delighted to discover that the American consul was Dr. Felix Petard, a surgeon with whom she had worked during the Civil War. When he told Barton and Margot that a battle was raging near the city of Haguenau, France, Barton at once asked if he could help them get there.

Petard had an idea. A busload of German-American tourists had been vacationing in France when the war broke out. Fearing the hatred of the French, these tourists were eager to reach the German-held city of Brumath, which was not far from Haguenau. Petard had already procured a bus for them, and there were seats available.

The following morning Barton and Margot were on the horse-drawn bus, with Petard himself riding alongside as their escort. An American flag had been fixed to the front of the bus to assure safe passage to Brumath. Upon reaching the first German outpost, however, the bus was stopped by a guard. Unfamiliar with the American flag, he refused to let the bus continue.

Otto von Bismarck was the first and most influential chancellor of the German Empire, which he helped to create in 1871.

While Petard was busy arguing with the guard Barton was struck with an idea. She tore off the red ribbon which she usually wore around her throat and took from her pocket a needle and spool of thread which she carried with her. Minutes later she was wearing upon her arm the insignia of the Red Cross. Approaching the guard, she pointed to her arm. His face lit up with understanding. "Ah, the Red Cross," he said. And with a gallant bow he waved the bus on.

Inside the bus to Brumath sat the first American citizen to wear the emblem of the Red Cross.

Barton's commitment to the Red Cross is in evidence in this photograph. When the photograph was originally taken in 1875, the brooch worn by Barton did not have a cross on it. She later painted a cross on the brooch and had the photograph reshot.

TEN

The Relief of Strasbourg

Unaware of the work of the Red Cross, German soldiers refused to let Barton and Margot into the embattled city of Haguenau. So the two women had to walk for hours through the woods and countryside that separated Haguenau from Brumath. Barton was determined not to let anything stop her from reaching the battlefront.

Darkness was starting to fall and there were rumbles of thunder. Suddenly it started to rain hard. Barton and Margot began to run toward the lights of a small town that they could see up ahead. After reaching one of the buildings, Barton knocked on a lighted window. A heavyset German woman looked out. Margot asked her if she would let them in, promising to pay the woman if they could lodge there for the night.

The woman admitted Barton and Margot, but as they were trying to dry themselves by the fire a group of neighbors crowded into the room and began to talk among themselves and eye the strangers, making Barton and Margot feel uneasy. Suddenly, there was a pounding on the door. The heavyset woman opened it, and in barged a group of German soldiers. The corporal in charge stepped forward and demanded to see Barton's and Margot's papers.

Unaware that they had been reported as spies, the two women handed the corporal their passports. While he was looking at the documents a huge, drunken sergeant bullied his way through the doorway and insisted on taking over the questioning. Drawing his sword, he shouted something in German and pushed Barton against the wall, putting his sword against her throat. Barton did not flinch. Instead, she stared into the man's eyes with dis-

After arriving in Strasbourg, Barton established a sewing center to help clothe the city's poor.

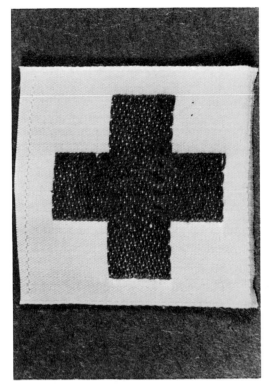

This was the armband worn by Barton while she performed relief work in Strasbourg.

dain. Sheepishly, the sergeant withdrew his sword, shouted a few commands to the corporal, and departed. The other soldiers trooped out after him.

Barton and Margot decided that they had better not sleep at the same time. Barton took the first watch while Margot lay down on their bed of straw. In the middle of the night, Barton heard a noise at the window. Looking out, she saw a young man, one of the neighbors she had seen earlier, trying to climb to the window.

"If you enter," Barton told him, "I will kill you if I can." She did not have a weapon, yet the young man seemed to understand her threat. He dropped to the ground and fled into the night.

Sometimes, getting to the front held as much danger as being at the battlesite.

The next day the two women returned to Brumath and were contacted by a messenger from the grand duchess of Baden. There was fighting in the German city of Karlsruhe, and the grand duchess wanted Barton and

(text continues on page 83)

A Red Cross worker cares for an injured soldier.

Napoleon III and Otto von Bismarck confer in 1871 after the Battle of Sedan, where the French forces suffered a disastrous defeat.

Napoleon III, shown here at Solferino, saw his empire fall in the war against Prussia.

After Napoleon III (third from right) surrendered to Bismarck at Sedan, France installed a republican government to carry on the war.

France's defeat in the Franco-Prussian War, which took place shortly after Austria's defeat in the Austro-Prussian War, led to a powerful and unified German Empire.

(text continued from page 78)

Margot to join her in taking care of the wounded. Barton and Margot were finally granted their wish and went to work with the Red Cross at the battlefront.

In late September 1870 the grand duchess received word that her husband, the duke of Baden, had taken Strasbourg. Much damage had been done to the French city, with thousands of homes damaged or destroyed and thousands of citizens killed or wounded. There were reports that the survivors were suffering terribly.

Barton and Margot departed at once for Strasbourg. With the help of other Red Cross volunteers, Barton made a survey of the city. She was soon organizing hospitals and kitchens and writing letters to raise funds for relief. The grand duchess was among those who contributed money. Barton realized, however, that more than charity was needed in rebuilding Strasbourg. The people must be motivated to help themselves. Developing what would later be a guiding principle for the Red Cross in her own country, Barton stressed the importance of rehabilitation. The people were paid wages to rebuild their city rather than having to rely on the charity of outsiders. Barton also hired several hundred women to make clothing for the rest of the population.

Barton's letter to a group of English contributers reveals her complete grasp of the health issues related to the project:

> My attempts to clothe the people of France have not been the result of a desire to improve the personal appearance ... it is to be hoped that few will die of outright hunger during the next six months, but thousands must fall pitiful victims to disease lurking in the only old rags, in which months ago, they escaped from fire and destruction.
>
> Disease is spread from one family to another, until thousands who are well today will rot with smallpox and be devoured by body lice before the end of August. Against the progress of these two scourges there is, I believe, no check but the destruction of all infected garments: hence the necessity for something to take their place. Excuse, sir, the plain and ugly terms which I have employed to express myself; the facts are plain and ugly.

Chancellor Bismarck later paid tribute to Barton by visiting her workrooms. This was an honor exceeded only by an event that took place in Strasbourg on Barton's 50th birthday, Christmas morning in 1871. Answering a knock at her door, she looked out to see a crowd of people standing beside a huge Christmas tree ablaze with candles. They had brought the tree to her as a gift, showing their gratitude for what she had done for them. By enabling the people to help themselves, Barton had given them back their self-respect.

Barton served as president of the American Red Cross for 23 years.

ELEVEN

The American Red Cross

After the Franco-Prussian War ended in triumph for Germany, with the annexation of the French provinces of Alsace and Lorraine, Barton continued to work for the Red Cross. From Strasbourg she went to Mertz in northern France, which had been overrun by German troops. There she aided a population so hungry that some of the people had eaten their own pets. Then she organized the relief of Paris, which had been devastated by a grueling siege. However, the unceasing toil and exposure to harsh conditions and illness finally had their effect. Barton was stricken with rheumatic fever. In October 1873, after resting for a little while in London, she returned to the United States.

Four years of convalescence followed. Afflicted with migraines and periods of blindness, Barton suffered from a nervous disorder so extreme that for a long time she could hardly stand by herself. Although she presented a brave front to the world, Barton's journals reveal that she suffered from periods of extreme melancholy. Able to perform brilliantly under the unrelenting pressure of war, she appeared to collapse, both physically and emotionally, once the pressure was off. Nursed by a Swiss girl, Minna Kupfer, who had been her aide in the Franco-Prussian War, Barton was treated at a sanatorium in Dansville, New York, in the northwest part of the state, where she would later buy a home.

One day in 1877, while Barton was reading about the impending war between Turkey and Russia, the news sparked memories of her work with the Red Cross. She wrote to Dr. Appia, expressing her desire to establish the Red Cross in America. Appia wrote back, filling her in on the progress of the Red

Barton's recuperative stay at a sanatorium in Dansville, New York, resulted in her buying a home in the area.

Cross since she had left Europe. Soon afterward she received a letter from Gustave Moynier, now president of the International Committee. Enclosed with his letter was another letter, to Rutherford B. Hayes, the president of the United States. This letter established Barton as the U.S. representative of the International Committee and asked that America sign the Geneva Treaty and organize a branch of the Red Cross.

Given a new mission, Barton arose from her sickbed and headed for Washington. She knew that she would have to build a groundwork of support before the president could be approached. Some of her old Washington contacts had died, including Senator Wilson, but Barton was a brilliant lobbyist who knew her way around the halls of Congress.

Despite her best efforts Barton received only a lukewarm reception

Having become a well-known international figure, Barton was invited to a New Year's Day reception at the Swiss Consulate in Washington, D.C., in 1878.

when she finally gave Moynier's letter to President Hayes. The president sent her to his attorney general, who sent her to his secretary of state, W. M. Evarts, who sent her to his assistant, Frederick W. Seward. Surprisingly, Seward knew something about the Red Cross. He was the son of a former secretary of state, William M. Seward, during whose administration, in 1866, a proposal to join the Red Cross had been considered. Frederick Seward dug out his father's old files and looked at them. Then he told Barton that the United States would never join the Red Cross.

Seward based his decision on the predominant view that the United States should isolate itself from other countries and that European meddling in U.S. affairs must be avoided. Joining the Red Cross would mean becoming involved in a treaty with foreign countries. In addition, Congress believed that the United States would not be fighting any wars in Europe, so there was no need for such a treaty.

Barton listened to Seward's arguments but did not think they made good sense. She decided she could win the support of Congress by showing that the Red Cross could be used to help people in times of peace as well as during a war. Should a natural disaster occur, a relief organization would be ready with doctors, nurses, and supplies.

After doing some research Barton found out that every year there was at least one major disaster in the United States caused by fire, flood, earthquake, or hurricane. Armed with her facts and arguments, she approached her friends in Congress as well as journalists who already supported the Red Cross.

When President James A. Garfield took office in 1881, Barton found him receptive to her cause. With no reason to suppose that congressional approval would now be denied, she began to organize the Red Cross in the United States even though her country had not yet signed the Geneva Treaty. On May 21, 1881, Barton called her followers and supporters to her apartment at 1326 I Street in Washington, thus establishing the American National Red Cross Society. Barton was elected the society's president. Three months later, on August 22, 1881, she organized the first local Red Cross chapter in the country, at Dansville; then came societies in Rochester and Syracuse, New York.

However, the United States was still not formally part of the International Committee of the Red Cross. As high as Barton's spirits had soared after having received the support of President Garfield, she was not yet able to see her dream realized. On July 2, 1881, President Garfield was shot and mortally wounded by an assassin. The president died two months later.

This turn of events meant that Bar-

Four months after being inaugurated as president in 1881, James A. Garfield was shot as he entered the Washington, D.C., train station. He died from his wounds two months later.

Vice-president Chester A. Arthur took over as president of the United States after James A. Garfield's death in September 1881.

ton had to start her lobbying work all over again with a new administration led by President Chester A. Arthur. To make matters more complex, she was troubled by the emergence of rival groups challenging the need for the Red Cross. These groups felt that the United States ought not to be a part of a European venture but should have a relief society of its own. They did not feel as Barton did—that only an international organization would provide the United States with the protection it would need in the future.

In the fall of 1881 fate intervened. A tremendous forest fire broke out in northern Michigan, leaving about 5,000 people homeless and many others badly injured. The new local Red Cross chapters at Dansville, Rochester, and Syracuse were ready to help out almost immediately with volunteers and supplies. Barton's home in Dansville, with the Red Cross flag hoisted above it, became a headquarters for volunteers from all over the country. For the first time in U.S. history an organization existed that was able to serve as a liaison between the victims of a natural disaster and those who wished to send contributions. The newspapers printed not only Barton's pleas for help but also excerpts from a pamphlet she had previously published about the Red Cross. In almost no time, Barton's organization had raised $80,000 to aid the victims of the fire.

Barton discovered during this time that she had a very able assistant to oversee Red Cross activities in the field. In 1876, during her long stay in Dansville, she had been visited by a young Iowa-born college student named Julian Hubbell. He had heard about Barton's activities during the Civil War, and he wanted to know how he could help her in her work. Barton told him to become a doctor, and Hubbell changed his major in college from chemistry to medicine. He was studying medicine at the University of Michigan when the great Michigan forest fire broke out. At Barton's request, he went to the scene of the fire to assess what supplies were needed and then stayed on to assist in their distribution.

A subsequent flood on the Ohio River gave the president and Congress another opportunity to see what the Red Cross could accomplish. Soon after, Barton was elated to hear that Congress had ratified the Geneva Treaty on March 16, 1882. President Arthur quickly signed the treaty into law.

Through this action, the United States became the 32nd member of the International Committee of the Red Cross— the last major nation in the world to ratify the Geneva Convention. When news of the signing reached Eu-

After joining the American National Red Cross, Dr. Julian Hubbell became Barton's devoted and indispensable chief aide.

rope there was great rejoicing. Gustave Moynier, president of the Red Cross, sent out an official bulletin stating that "without the energy and perseverance of this remarkable woman, Clara Barton, we should not for a long time have had the pleasure of seeing the Red Cross received in the United States."

Once her struggle for acceptance of the Red Cross was finally over, Barton spent eight months in 1883 as the superintendent of the Sherborn State Prison for Women in Massachusetts. Urged to take the position by her old friend, General Benjamin F. Butler, who had become the governor of Massachusetts, Barton continued to work to improve the self-respect and dignity of all those with whom she came into contact. In her writings she stated:

> I believe the record of my last month at Sherborn shows not a single punishment among between 300 and 400 women. They grew to feel that the only hurt of their punishment was the pain it gave me. When I met them for the last night in the chapel, and told them we should not meet again, and invited each to come and bid me goodbye ... the tears that went over my hands as I held theirs for the last time were harder for me than all the eight months' work I had done among them.

Barton resumed her Red Cross work the following year when news came of tremendous flooding on the Ohio and Mississippi Rivers. This flooding, which was destined to leave 7,000 homeless, was so severe that Barton and her field agent, Julian Hubbell, found the city of Cincinnati under water. People had to be rescued from third-story windows by boats. To bring relief to the victims of the flood, Barton decided to charter a boat herself—a Red Cross relief ship called the *Josh V. Throop*. For four months it sailed up and down the swollen rivers, bringing aid to the victims and volunteers working to rebuild homes.

When Barton's river work was finally finished she had sailed over 8,000 miles with the *Throop*. Once more she had worn herself out and was feeling ill and exhausted. But no sooner had she arrived home to enjoy a well-earned rest

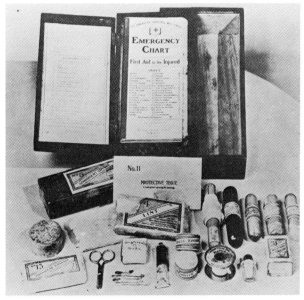

The first aid kit was made a part of the medical world thanks to Barton.

than she found a message from Europe waiting for her: A Red Cross conference was being held in Geneva, and the new American National Red Cross Society was invited to send a representative. Barton at once called upon Secretary of State Frelinghuysen and asked him to name a delegate. Frelinghuysen wanted to appoint Barton, but she said that she was feeling ill and was too tired. Frelinghuysen responded: "Regarding your illness—you have had too much fresh water, Miss Barton. I recommend salt—and shall appoint you."

Salt water, of course, meant an ocean voyage. And as had so often happened with Barton in the past, she recovered immediately.

By the time Barton was in her sixties, she was just beginning to involve herself in some of her most important projects.

TWELVE

The Red Cross in Action

Clara Barton was 63 years old when she served as the only woman delegate to the International Red Cross Conference in Geneva. Accompanying Barton were two other American delegates: Adolphus S. Solomon, vice president of the American National Red Cross; and Judge Joseph Sheldon, a key figure in the American organization. Sheldon, who was the keynote speaker at the conference, made quite a well-received speech, which paid specific tribute to Barton for having brought the United States into the Red Cross.

During the conference, Barton's idea of employing the Red Cross during times of peace to relieve the victims of natural disaster was adopted into the organization's charter. Called "The American Amendment" by Julian Hubbell, who also attended the conference, Barton's idea was initially met with opposition by those who felt that the Red Cross should remain an exclusively wartime organization. Gustave Moynier, for one, declared that "to use a flag [the Red Cross emblem] which has a legal significance determined by the Convention of Geneva for undertakings of a different character from those for which it is intended is undoubtedly wrong." However, time has shown Barton's concept of a peacetime Red Cross to be a good one.

Between 1881 and 1904 Barton continued to raise money for the Red Cross as well as help to administer it. She also gave lectures, wrote a 700-page book about the Red Cross, founded a National First Aid Society to help accident victims, and lobbied for women's rights. In fact, she was a vice-president and featured speaker at the First International Women's Suffrage Conference in Washington, D.C.

Barton's most important contribu-

Barton took an active role in fighting for the advancement of women's rights by speaking at rallies and suffrage meetings.

tion in her later years was to shape and build the American National Red Cross. In this regard she demonstrated not only a remarkable skill at publicizing her cause but also a talent for bringing into her organization exceptional people from all walks of life. Among these people were Judge Sheldon, his wife, Abby Barker, and Barton's own nephew, Stephen Barton, who worked with Sheldon to put together the original charter for the Red Cross. Dr. Joseph Gardner and his wife, Enola Lee, were in charge of distributing supplies at the scene of a disaster. To handle the business part of the organization,

Barton was able to enlist the help of George Pullman, founder of the Pullman Company, which made train carriages. He was introduced to Barton by his partner, Robert Lincoln, son of President Lincoln and a strong supporter of the Red Cross.

Surrounded by people of integrity and ability, Barton remained active in the field, visiting disaster sites herself and always working directly with the victims. Almost every year brought a new disaster for which the Red Cross was needed.

In 1888, for example, Barton assisted the people of Jacksonville, Florida, who were stricken with an outbreak of yellow fever. This epidemic marked the first use of trained Red Cross nurses.

In the spring of 1889 a severe rainstorm caused extensive flooding in parts of Pennsylvania, leaving the city of Johnstown under as much as 13 feet of water. Several days later a dam broke in the mountains near the city, and a 30-foot-high wave bore down on Johnstown, killing more than 2,000 people and destroying millions of dollars' worth of property. Barton arrived in Johnstown five days later, on the first train that could get through. For five months she lived and worked in a tent, using an empty dry goods box as her desk. From this humble headquarters she organized crews of men to clean up the wreckage and teams of women to distribute clothing. Not only were the people of Johnstown fed and housed but care was also provided for the starving livestock.

In 1892 famine swept Russia. Since Russia had exerted pressure on Britain and France to prevent them from recognizing the Confederate South during the Civil War, many grateful Americans were anxious to help the Russian people. Farmers in Iowa dispatched hundreds of carloads of corn to New York in care of the Red Cross. The corn was subsequently distributed in Russia by Julian Hubbell. Although this relief was small, it had a major impact: it served to introduce to the American people the concept of foreign aid.

The Dansville Society of the Red Cross put out this appeal for help for the victims of the 1881 Michigan forest fires.

A marker at one of the Michigan forest fire sites states about the Red Cross, "This was the first disaster relief furnished by this great organization."

In 1893 a hurricane swept across the Sea Islands off the coast of South Carolina. Almost 5,000 people were drowned, and 30,000 were left homeless. When no other organization came forward to help, President Grover Cleveland personally appealed to the Red Cross for assistance.

In providing relief to the Sea Islanders, Barton kept the focus on rehabilitation. The entire relief fund raised amounted to $30,500, or about a dollar apiece for the 30,000 people who went homeless for ten months. Yet the rehabilitation effort was successful because Barton insisted that the people work on rebuilding their homes as a condition for receiving food rations. A further requirement was that each house had to have a vegetable garden.

Wielding clubs to ward off those who might interfere with their effort, Turkish Red Cross workers carry away victims of the Armenian Massacres.

More than 2,000 people lost their lives in the 1889 Johnstown, Pennsylvania, floods.

At first the inhabitants protested that there was no use in planting a garden because their pigs would eat all of the produce. However, after the gardens were planted, they produced crops of such richness, variety, and abundance that Barton wrote: "It was nearly as difficult for a pedestrian to make his way on the narrow sidewalks of Beaufort because of piled-up vegetables as it had been in October to pass through the streets because of the hungry, idle men and women."

In February 1893 Barton received a cable from Turkey saying she was needed to help the survivors of a religious war. The victims were Christian Armenians living within a mostly Mus-lim empire. Many of the Muslim Turks wanted to eliminate the entire Armenian population from Turkey. Since Turkey was a member of the Geneva Convention, however, the country was forced to abide by the Convention's rules and help to provide relief for the Armenians. So, at the age of 72, Barton called upon Tevfik Pasha, the Turkish minister of foreign affairs, and set out with her forces to bring relief to thousands of towns and villages that had no other hope of receiving aid. Separate expeditions were led by Julian Hubbell and a second Red Cross doctor, Ira Harris. Part of the task undertaken by these medical teams involved rounding up oxen and other work an-

The American National Red Cross supplied relief and helped with the rehabilitation of the victims of the Sea Islands disaster in 1893.

imals that had been driven up into the mountains, so that the war-torn fields could be replanted. This took place along routes so infested with thieves that at one point the Red Cross hired a bandit chief to serve as a guide and escort for its workers.

Barton remained in Constantinople (the largest city in Turkey, now called Istanbul) with George Pullman, who handled the accounts for the distribution of relief funds. All in all, Barton and the Red Cross spent ten months in Turkey helping the victims of the religious war and aiding 10,000 people who had been stricken by epidemics of typhoid, typhus, dysentery, and smallpox.

In 1897 the United States became concerned with the plight of thousands of Cuban nationalists who had been herded into concentration camps as political prisoners by their Spanish overlords. The Red Cross was chosen to dispense funds for the relief of these prisoners, with Barton's nephew, Stephen Barton, chairing the Central Cuban Relief Committee.

On February 15, 1898, the U.S. battleship *Maine* was blown up in the harbor of Havana, Cuba, taking the lives of 260 men. Barton was there to help the survivors. On April 25 the United States declared war on Spain—which controlled Cuba and the Philippines—the U.S. Navy laid siege to Cuba, and the Spanish-American War began. Between April and August of 1898 battles were fought in the Philippines and Puerto Rico as well as in Cuba. This war provided the first opportunity for the American Red Cross to give medical aid in wartime.

Among the wounded men whom Barton treated during the Spanish-American War were the Rough Riders, the volunteer cavalry regiment led by Colonel Theodore Roosevelt, who in 1901 became president of the United States. On one occasion Roosevelt himself emerged from a nearby jungle, where he and his men had been fighting, and entered Barton's Red Cross headquarters, requesting food and supplies for his men. Barton wrote about the encounter:

> After a few moments conversation he said, "I have some sick men with the regiment who refuse to leave it. They need such delicacies as you have here which I am ready to pay for out of my own pocket. Can I buy them from the Red Cross?"

98

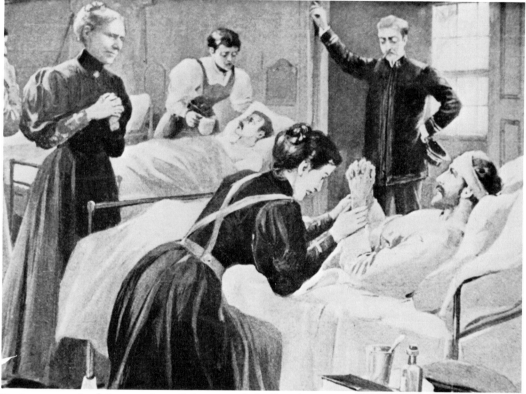

Barton supervised the nursing of the wounded after the Maine *explosion.*

"Not for a million dollars," said Dr. Gardner.

"But my men need these things," he said, his tone and face expressing anxiety, "I think a great deal of my men. I am proud of them."

"And we know they are proud of you, Colonel, but we can't sell Red Cross supplies."

"Then how can I get them? I must have proper food for my sick men," he said.

"Just ask for them, Colonel."

"Oh," he said, his face lighting up with a bright smile, "then I do ask for them."

When Dr. Gardner asked where to send the supplies, Roosevelt thundered that he would take them along if the Red Cross would provide him with a sack.

> Before we had recovered from our surprise, the incident was closed by the future President of the U.S. slinging the big sack over his shoulders, striding off, and out of sight through the jungle.

When the United States finally ended the war by winning the Battle of Santiago de Cuba, the first ship to enter the harbor of Cuba's capital city of Havana was a Red Cross relief ship, the *Texas*. At its helm stood the 77-year-old Clara Barton.

At the age of 83, Barton resigned from her post as president of the American National Red Cross Society.

THIRTEEN

Final Battles

Not all of Barton's later years proved to be as smooth sailing as her triumphant entry into Cuba. The ship on which Barton sailed into Havana had been outfitted by the New York chapter of the Red Cross. This powerful branch of the organization rose to challenge Barton's authority. Led by an ambitious and capable society woman named Mabel Boardman, the New York chapter was a professionally run organization whose leaders became increasingly critical of Barton's methods of administration. They also believed that for the organization to grow, it must be placed under the guidance of those who had wealth or social prestige.

On September 8, 1900, a tornado and a tidal wave swept over the city of Galveston, Texas. Barton did her last field work for the Red Cross among the corpse-strewn ruins of that city, then returned to Washington to face a torrent of criticism because no specific procedure had been enforced for the distribution of Red Cross funds. A Red Cross board of control, which had just been established by the federal government, pressed for certain reforms. Among them was the demand that money for the American National Red Cross be paid to the organization's treasurer and disbursed only by him.

Stung by the criticism of their leader, Barton's supporters responded by doing away with the board of control and replacing it with their own board of directors. They also increased the powers of the president. This led to open division within the Red Cross, with members of the Boardman group calling for Barton's resignation. They felt that the Red Cross could grow only if Barton stepped aside.

The hostility between the two factions finally reached such a pitch that Barton's integrity was called into question. There were charges of misappropriated funds, accusations that she failed to delegate responsibility, and complaints that records of disbursements were missing. Barton's supporters recommended that in order for Barton to clear her name she submit to a public investigation. They stipulated, however, that the study be con-

ducted by the Red Cross rather than by a congressional committee. It was true that Barton had not always kept accurate records, yet had often used her own funds for relief. She was devastated by these developments.

Eventually, all of the charges were dropped, and Barton's reputation was restored. In 1902 she received a vote of confidence in her leadership by being elected president of the Red Cross for

Always interested in meeting those who shared her passion for nursing, Barton visited a group of graduates at the Blockley Hospital School of Nursing in Philadelphia, Pennsylvania, in 1902.

life. Yet this move did not end the struggle for power, and the Boardman group soon gained a powerful ally in President Theodore Roosevelt. They succeeded in convincing the president that Barton was doing a poor job. In 1903 Roosevelt and his cabinet resigned from an honorary Red Cross board of consultation, a move that so upset Barton that at one point she contemplated leaving the country. She held on to the presidency of the Red Cross until 1904. Then, at the age of 83, she resigned from her post, worn out by the battles within the organization.

In the end, the Boardman forces gained control. In June 1905, a year after Barton's resignation, the Red Cross was reorganized under a new congressional charter that created the institution as it exists today. The new charter provided that the Red Cross consist of a central committee of 18 members, six to be elected by Red Cross board members, six to be chosen by the state and territorial Red Cross societies, and six, including the chairman of the central committee, to be appointed by the president of the United States. The records of the Red

Barton's home at Glen Echo, Maryland, served as the American National Red Cross headquarters from 1897 to 1904.

Clara Barton dines with guests at her home in Glen Echo.

International Red Cross Medal

Pansy carved from amethyst

Iron Cross of Imperial Germany

Cross would be audited by the War Department.

After leaving the Red Cross Barton went on to create the National First Aid Society, which assisted accident victims. She spent her last years at her home in Glen Echo, Maryland, which also served as national headquarters for the Red Cross. Her home was built with lumber that had been left over from the rehabilitation in Johnstown. She was cared for by her personal physician, Dr. Julian Hubbell, who also lived at Glen Echo, directing the development of the medical resources of the Red Cross.

During her last years Barton had time to pursue her interests in astrology, religion, and spiritualism. She was often seen weeding her garden, wearing on her chest the medals awarded

Fond of wearing the many decorations she was awarded over the years, Barton claimed, "They do brighten up the old dress."

Cross of Imperial Russia

Smoky topaz with pearls

Masonic emblem

to her for a life of service—a medal from the Red Cross in Geneva, the Royal Jewel given to her by the grand duchess of Baden, a scarlet topaz brooch from the empress of Germany, a silver and red enamel medal from the czar of Russia, and many others. She remained active until her death from double pneumonia on April 12, 1912, when she was 90 years old.

By nature Barton was sensitive and shy. She preferred to avoid arguments whenever she could. Yet her friend Julian Hubbell once noted that, when pressed on any subject, she could say more on the point than almost anyone. Blessed with a keen, scholarly mind, she was also very independent. For the most part, she did not enjoy working with established groups, such as the U.S. Sanitary Commission. Her preference was to strike out on her own.

A tremendous humanitarian who was always conscious of propriety, she nevertheless defied the usual way of doing things when it presented obstacles rather than solutions. Hubbell said of her that she not only sympathized with suffering, she herself suffered. Sensitive to criticism, and often doubtful of her own self-worth, she was able to overcome the melancholy streak in her nature when she was bringing comfort to others. At such times the normally shy and ladylike ex-schoolteacher could run through a hail of bullets to do her job. She brought to her work not only a rare gift for organiza-

Mabel Boardman eventually won control of the American National Red Cross in 1904.

tion but a persistence and determination that could overcome any obstacle in her path.

The life of a person with vision is often one of struggle, of constantly fighting the status quo. Barton's life was filled with her battles for progress. She was one of the first to see the need in Bordentown for free public school education, to demonstrate that women could work alongside men in a government office, to realize that nursing must be done at the battlefront and that female nurses could be employed to do it, to create an agency to locate missing soldiers. She was among the first in her country to comprehend the importance of having the Red Cross in the United States, and she worked to make her countrymen understand this. She may have been the first person to realize that the International Red Cross could be used to aid people in times of peace. Following her lead, the United States started to help other nations with foreign aid. Whenever there was an obstacle to success, Barton overcame it.

Barton is largely remembered today for having founded the American Red Cross. Yet her accomplishments have served much more than just one country. In making sure that *all* victims of wars and natural disasters will be aided by trained volunteers, she became in fact a truly international figure.

The headquarters for the nearly 2 million volunteers who serve in the American National Red Cross is located in Washington, D.C.

FURTHER READING

Barton, Clara. *The Story of My Childhood*. New York: Arno Press, 1980.

Boylston, Helen Dore. *Clara Barton, Founder of the American Red Cross*. New York: Random House, 1955.

Brockett, L. P., and Mary C. Vaughan. *Woman's Work in the Civil War: A Record of Heroism, Patriotism and Patience*. Boston: R. H. Curran, 1967.

Deming, Richard. *Heroes of the International Red Cross*. New York: Meredith Press, 1969.

Fishwick, Marshall W., and the editors of Silver Burdett. *Illustrious Americans: Clara Barton*. Morristown, NJ: Silver Burdett, 1966.

Hurd, Charles. *The Compact History of the American Red Cross*. New York: Hawthorn Books, 1959.

Levenson, Dorothy. *The First Book of the Civil War*. New York: Franklin Watts, 1977.

Ross, Ishbel. *Angel of the Battlefield, The Life of Clara Barton*. New York: Harper & Brothers, 1956.

CHRONOLOGY

Dec. 25, 1821	Clara Barton is born in North Oxford, Massachusetts
1832–34	Nurses her brother, David
1839	Earns her teaching certificate and begins teaching
1850	Enrolls at the Clinton Liberal Institute for female teachers
1852	Establishes free public school in Bordentown, New Jersey
1854	Begins working as a clerk in the Patent Office in Washington, D.C.
1861	The Civil War begins; Barton begins nursing Union soldiers
1862	Returns home to nurse her dying father
	Receives permission to nurse the wounded at the battlefront
Sept. 1862	Battle of Antietam
Dec. 1862	Battle of Fredericksburg
1863	Red Cross founded in Geneva, Switzerland
	Battle of Spotsylvania
1864–65	Serves as superintendent of nurses for the Army of the James
April 9, 1865	Civil War ends
1865	Barton begins a nationwide search for missing soldiers
1869	Sails to Europe
	Meets with representatives of the Red Cross
1870–71	Works with the Red Cross during the Franco-Prussian War
Oct. 1873	Returns to the United States
1881	Establishes the American Red Cross Society
March 16, 1882	Congress ratifies the Geneva Treaty, enabling the United States to join the International Committee of the Red Cross
1889	Organizes relief efforts after the Johnstown flood
1898	Helps victims of the Spanish-American War
1902	Elected president of the Red Cross for life
1904	Resigns from the Red Cross
1905	Founds the National First Aid Society
April 12, 1912	Dies of double pneumonia

INDEX

Leni Hamilton holds a bachelor's degree from Brandeis University and a master of fine arts degree from the Yale University School of Drama. *The Fortress*, her historical drama about Benedict Arnold, won the New Jersey Women's Playwriting Award in 1980. Several other Hamilton plays, including *Piece of Mind, Second Sight,* and *Poetic License,* have received off-Broadway productions. Hamilton is currently employed as a manuscript analyst for a New York City–based literary agency.

❖   ❖   ❖

Matina S. Horner is president of Radcliffe College and associate professor of psychology and social relations at Harvard University. She is best known for her studies of women's motivation, achievement, and personality development. Dr. Horner serves on several national boards and advisory councils, including those of the National Science Foundation, Time Inc., and the Women's Research and Education Institute. She earned her B. A. from Bryn Mawr College and Ph.D. from the University of Michigan, and holds honorary degrees from many colleges and universities, including Mount Holyoke, Smith, Tufts, and the University of Pennsylvania.

PICTURE CREDITS